GLORY ROSE:
A Story of Shattered Vows and Renewed Passion.

Felix Shaba (PhD)

DEDICATION

Dedicated to the memory of Ada's mother, Grace Ngozi. This novel honours your sacrifices, the steadfast love you provided to your children, and the values you instilled in them. Your memory will always remain in their hearts, cherished with profound love and eternal gratitude.

DISCLAIMER

This is a work of fiction. Names, characters, places, and incidents are either products of the author's imagination or are used fictitiously. Any resemblance to actual persons, living or dead, events, or locales is purely coincidental.

The views and opinions expressed by the characters do not reflect those of the author or any affiliated entities. The author does not intend to offend, defame, or harm any individual, group, or institution.

Chapter 1:

A Divine Encounter

The evening at the University of Ibadan Christian Fellowship was filled with a palpable sense of epiphany as students gathered for their midweek service. An undeniable feeling of transcendence permeated the air, creating a sensation that lifted everyone present beyond the ordinary into a realm of spiritual connection. The atmosphere within the chapel that Wednesday night was charged with an almost electric energy; it felt as though each person was soaked in the euphoria of the moment. Some students stood with arms outstretched, their faces lifted toward the heavens, joining their voices in a fervent chorus. Others were overwhelmed with emotion, rolling on the floor, tears streaming down their faces in deep, agonised supplication. A few moved about in silent prayer, lost in their own world, while some remained still, as if waiting for something greater to envelop them. The entire room buzzed with spiritual intensity, as though every soul present was caught up in a divine power they couldn't fully comprehend.

The night began with a powerful praise and worship session that set the stage for the message. The energy was vibrant, yet an undercurrent of expectancy lingered as if everyone knew that something great was imminent. The praise and worship served as a prelude, drawing everyone into a deep connection with God, but it was the sermon that conveyed the true weight of the evening's focus.

The sermon on forgiveness struck like a sword at the students' hearts and souls. As the preacher spoke, the weight of the message seemed to cut through the euphoria of the moment, reaching deep into the personal struggles and unhealed wounds of many present. For some, it served as a sharp reminder of unresolved bitterness and grudges they had carried for far too long. The truth of God's call to forgive, regardless of the pain they had endured, felt like an open wound being pressed upon, evoking discomfort and the potential for healing. The message was challenging in its starkness, urging the students to reconsider the burden of their own bitterness and how it hinders their spiritual journey growth.

For others, the message was an invitation to reconcile with God, acknowledging the times when they too had fallen short in forgiving others. The students were compelled to confront their own hearts—no longer able to hide behind the euphoria of worship but instead standing face-to-face with the reality of what it truly means to forgive as Christ forgave. The sermon cut through their defences, leaving them to grapple with the true essence of forgiveness.

It was a moment of deep introspection and transformation, where the students had the opportunity to let go of old hurts, experience healing, and embrace the freedom that comes with forgiveness, even when it felt impossible.

Yetunde held her Bible close to her chest, her face still flushed from the intensity of the service. As she moved towards the exit of the chapel, the gentle evening breeze caressed her skin, sending a ripple of cool air through her body, causing her hair to stand on end. The message had resonated deeply, evoking a strong emotional response within her. Each word echoed in her heart, and all she desired was to go straight to her hostel and fully absorb the weight of a sermon she had never viewed from the perspective taken by the invited preacher.

Meanwhile, Afolabi stood by the door, watching intently as Yetunde gathered her belongings—her Bible, notebook, and pen. Without blinking, he observed every move she made. For weeks now, he had been captivated by her, unable to resist stealing glances. Everything about her seemed to enthrall him. Her round face, soft cheeks, and almond-shaped, dark eyes were striking, while the dimples on her upper and lower lips only added to her allure. However, it wasn't just her physical beauty that enchanted him; there was something deeper, something far more profound, that kept him riveted.

The depth of her devotion during worship left him mesmerised. He watched in awe as she raised her hands in praise with genuine sincerity, her eyes closed as if speaking directly to God. He admired the subtle tilt of her head as she absorbed every word the pastor spoke, her full attention focused on the message. When she sang, her graceful, effortless dance steps seemed to radiate an inner joy. There was an unmistakable aura around her—a captivating blend of resilience and calmness—that stirred something powerful within him. It was more than admiration; it was an emotion he could not quite define or understand.

She was not in her customary rose-pink outfit, the one she often wore on Wednesdays when she came straight from class to avoid being late. Instead, tonight, Yetunde wore a lemon-coloured dress that seemed to brighten the entire room, enhancing her natural charm in a way that caught Afolabi off guard. As the service drew to a close, a powerful urge surged within him to approach her. He was unsure whether it was the subtle push of unseen forces or the result of his own growing courage, but what he did know was that he could not let the moment pass—the time for silent admiration must end. He had to act, even if his heart pounded at the thought of it.

As Yetunde turned to leave the chapel, Afolabi moved forward, discreetly clearing his throat. "Sister Yetunde?" His voice exuded a sense of composure, yet a subtle undertone of unease punctuated his utterance of her name, as if he were savouring it with newfound curiosity. It felt as though he was calling her name for the first time, relishing it with an unfamiliar intrigue that both fascinated and unsettled him. Everything about her felt magnified in that brief moment—the gentle sway of her hair and the grace in her movements. He could not quite pinpoint why this interaction felt so critical, but something within him knew it was.

Yetunde looked up, her expression filled with surprise. Unaware of Afolabi's presence until now, she momentarily paused, her gaze carefully studying his face as if trying to place him among the familiar faces in the chapel. "Yes, brother, good evening?" she replied, her voice polite but laced with a hint of caution. As she spoke, she instinctively cradled her Bible closer to her chest, a small gesture of comfort in this unexpected encounter. The warm glow of the lamp hanging over the chapel door illuminated her, casting a soft halo around her. Her rich, deep brown skin glowed with a smooth and even complexion, enhancing her natural beauty.

"Um, allow me to introduce myself," Afolabi said, his voice slightly unsteady as he gathered his thoughts. "My name is Afolabi, and I'm a final-year student in the Computer Science Department." He paused, searching for the right words; a sudden wave of nervousness swept over him. "I've, um, noticed you around during fellowship," he continued, his gaze steadying on hers. "Your insights during Bible studies are consistently thought-provoking. You have a way of expressing ideas that makes everyone think more deeply about the message.

Yetunde's expression softened at the compliment, a spark of warmth breaking through her initial caution. "Thank you, Brother Afolabi. We return all the glory to God," she replied, her voice steady and composed, reflecting her deep-rooted faith. She offered him a faint smile, though her eyes remained guarded, betraying a mix of curiosity and hesitation within her. The soft light from the lamp above cast gentle highlights on her features, accentuating her grace as she continued, "It's nice to meet you."

There was a moment of silence, stretching out and seeming to linger like a thick fog. Afolabi sensed her hesitation and observed how she held herself a bit more tightly, as if bracing for a conversation she was not entirely eager to engage in. Yet, a flicker of determination ignited within him. With a blend of resolve and gentleness, he leaned slightly closer, lowering his voice to convey sincerity.

"I was wondering if you'd be interested in discussing some of the topics we covered this evening," he began, his eyes locked onto hers, searching for any sign of openness.

"Your perspective is always so insightful, and I would love to hear more of your thoughts."

Yetunde fidgeted nervously, scanning the auditorium as if searching for a way out. There was something about Afolabi that made him seem genuinely sincere—perhaps it was the warmth in his eyes, the kindness in his voice, or his quiet confidence—it felt authentic and inviting. However, this sudden and unexpected attention brought with it a certain unease. She was unfamiliar with the situation, uncertain about his intention.

"That's very kind of you, Brother Afolabi," she finally said, carefully selecting her words. "However, I don't think I have anything more to add beyond what I already shared during the fellowship. Today's message calls for more prayer and personal reflection than for further discussion."

Afolabi was taken aback by her words, his face momentarily revealing disappointment, but he quickly concealed it behind a warm smile, nodding as if he understood her hesitancy. "I apologise if I've made you feel uncomfortable," he said, his voice steady despite the unease he sensed radiating from her. "If you ever feel like picking up this conversation again—or if you just need someone to talk to—please feel free to reach out to me," he offered, momentarily forgetting that he had been the one who initiated this discussion.

Yetunde nodded, maintaining her polite smile, though a hint of uncertainty flashed in her eyes. "Thank you for your kind words," she said, "I'll keep that in mind!"

Afolabi stepped back, allowing her some space; his heart felt slightly weighed down but remained filled with optimism. "Have a wonderful evening, Sister Yetunde," he said with a warm smile.

"You too, Brother Afolabi," she replied, her voice soft yet resolute as she turned to leave. Her movements were deliberate, a blend of grace and caution, her mind shielded against the lingering emotions stirred by their encounter.

As Afolabi watched her walk away, a storm of emotions swirled within him: respect for her calm composure and a quiet sense of disappointment. He could sense the hesitation in her every movement, the subtle wall she maintained, intriguing and frustrating him at the same time. It only fueled his desire to know more, to peel back the layers of mystery she wore so effortlessly. Each step she took felt like an invitation–a puzzle he was determined to solve. Time was of no concern to him; he was resolute in his intention to delve deeper into her world. He was convinced their meeting was no mere coincidence, and he was prepared to wait, however long it took, to uncover the true purpose behind their connection.

Afolabi could not sleep that night. Everywhere he looked, Yetunde's image seemed to surround him. He replayed their conversation over and over again, analysing each word, mentally critiquing things he had said that he shouldn't have and lamenting the things he wished he had voiced instead. This was a lady he had admired for a while; how could he miss the golden opportunity to establish a concrete friendship with her from the start? The weight of his unspoken thoughts hung heavily in the air, suffocating him with regret.

When he could no longer endure the restless turmoil, he fell to his knees, seeking solace in prayer. The stillness of the night enveloped him as he whispered fervent words, pouring out his heart to God, who understood the depths of his yearning. Afterwards, he picked up his diary and scribbled, "Yetunde, you are my wife!" The bold declaration felt both exhilarating and startling, a promise to himself that he was determined to pursue. Tossing the diary aside, he stretched out on the bed, his heart still throbbing with the sweet sound of Yetunde's name echoing in his thoughts. In the midst of the tense silence, dawn crept into the room, its golden light spilling across the walls like a quiet declaration, suggesting the beginning of a new day.

Afolabi momentarily forgot his travails and went about his tasks with renewed vigour. He detested disappointing his clients with every fibre of his being. Additionally, his final-year project was at a critical stage, demanding his full attention. He was in the final stretch of his work when something popped up on his screen. His fingers hesitated for a moment before he opened it, expecting nothing more than a trivial update. But what he saw left him breathless. The image staring back at him was the same one he had sketched the night before—a rough sketch of Yetunde.

To his astonishment, the drawing seemed almost alive. Her broad, semi-round nose stood out prominently, commanding attention as if she were staring right back at him. The longer he gazed at the image, the more her features appeared to animate, flooding his mind with vivid flashes of her laughter, her grace, and the quiet warmth she possessed. Within moments, the once simple sketch transformed into a striking and almost lifelike portrait, now illuminated as the background on his screen. It felt as though her essence had been captured in a way that was both exhilarating and unsettling, leaving him with a sense of awe—and an undeniable unease.

A wave of realisation washed over him, prompting him to shut down his system and stare blankly at the ceiling. This was his manner whenever he was deep in thought. After a brief period of contemplation, he took a shower, dressed in one of his finest clothes, and went out. He was so conscious of his appearance that he strolled leisurely along the street. This was a sharp contrast to his brisk and often hurried walk, which usually left him sweating in the process.

Afolabi waved down a taxi right outside the University of Ibadan gate in Agbowo. He sat with a relaxed and calm posture. Sliding into the back seat, he nodded at the driver and asked him to head toward University College Hospital (UCH). The day felt effortless; the traffic was light, and Afolabi's mind wandered to the steady bustle of the city as the taxi made its way through Bodija towards the Secretariat, offering a welcome contrast to the hectic pace of the past few days. Before long, he found himself on Queen Elizabeth Road, where student nurses hurried about, engaged in their routines. Yet, none of them captured his attention. However, as he looked up, he spotted the disappearing figure of a student nurse in the distance. There was something familiar about her, judging by her back view.

He quickened his steps, excitement bubbling within him as he closed the distance, his heart pounding against his chest in anticipation of an encounter. But as he drew nearer, his enthusiasm swiftly transformed into confusion. The figure turned, revealing a frail, gaunt lady who bore no resemblance to Yetunde. Disbelief washed over him, and he rubbed his eyes, trying to assure himself he was not seeing double. Amidst his distraction, he stepped on the tip of his agbada, causing him to lose his footing, tripping, and stumbling before he could regain his balance.

"JESUS..." Several voices shouted at the same time.

In an instant, the lady sprang to his side, effortlessly helping him up. Her speed and strength were remarkable, but what Afolabi found most puzzling was the unexpected contrast between the tenderness of her palm and the firmness of her grip as she steadied him.

"Are you hurt?" she asked, her voice sweet and soothing, laced with genuine concern. In her eagerness to ensure his safety, she completely disregarded the traditional male-female boundary, her instinctive kindness shining through.

"I'm alright," he replied, his voice husky as he dusted himself off, trying to regain some semblance of composure.

"Are you sure?" she asked, detaching herself from him even as her concern still lingered in the air.

"Yes, I am." he insisted, though a hint of doubt remained in his voice.

"Don't be too sure for now because you may not feel any pain at the moment until much later," she counselled. "I advise you to forget wherever you were headed, return home, and take a hot bath to rest. It'll certainly help," she reiterated.

Afolabi turned to her again, studying her features more intently. While she resembled Yetunde in some ways, with a few familiar traits, she lacked the height and voluptuousness that had made Yetunde so striking. Though she was kind and caring, this lady felt like a mere shadow of the person he truly longed for.

"But…but, why did she appear so frail and gaunt in my eyes?" Afolabi pondered in his heart, feeling confused and concerned, yet with no one to answer.

"I'm very grateful for your kindness," he said, his voice nearly a whisper yet tinged with sincerity. "Never mind," she replied with a bright smile, her eyes sparkling with warmth. "I should get going—I'm almost late for my lectures!" With that, she turned and hurried off, her footsteps quickening, leaving him with no chance to express his gratitude one last time.

Afolabi glanced at himself again, dismayed to find his prized white Agbada rumpled and stained with dirt. He brushed it off as much as he could, feeling embarrassed. With a sigh, he turned to leave, hoping to escape unnoticed. He had just taken a few steps when he came face to face with Yetunde, who widened her eyes in surprise upon seeing him. She was accompanied by two of her fellow student nurses.

Yetunde's gaze dropped to the stains marring his pristine white agbada, and a worried frown crossed her face. "Afolabi, what happened?" she asked, her voice laced with genuine concern. Momentarily forgetting her friends, she stepped closer, the worry evident in her expression eyes.

"Did you fall down?" she asked, her voice filled with genuine concern as she stepped closer, her eyes searching his for any sign of distress.

Afolabi nodded, feeling quite awkward. "I should be leaving now," he murmured, keen to escape the scrutiny of her gaze.

"Wait a moment." She grasped Afolabi's left hand and examined it closely. The warmth of her touch sent a shiver up his spine, captivating him with her focus. "Kate, please bring me your first aid kit," she called to one of her friends. "He has an open wound on the tip of his little finger. If something isn't done soon, it could get infected," she added, her voice tinged with concern.

Despite his reluctance to be fussed over, Afolabi had no choice but to submit to their orders. A part of him resisted, yet another part secretly enjoyed Yetunde's tender touches as she tended to his injury. The way she carefully cleaned the wound and bandaged his finger felt comforting, almost intimate.

Once the three ladies had finished treating him and cleaning the dirt from his agbada, they instructed him not to disturb his finger for a while.

"See you on Sunday at fellowship," Yetunde said, her voice brightening as they bid him goodbye.

"Thank you so much," Afolabi murmured, his words slipping out with sincere appreciation. "I truly lack the words to express my gratitude."

At that moment, he felt as though he had won a trophy, her concern and care wrapping around him like a warm embrace. Those words were more than reassuring; they made him forget the pain in his finger and the messy state of his agbada, leaving him buoyed by the connection they had forged. In that quiet moment, as the ladies tended to him, the joy of seeing Yetunde filled his heart, making his journey to UCH worthwhile. Despite the fall, he realised it had brought Yetunde closer to him, and her soothing care had turned the whole experience into something memorable—a moment of unexpected comfort amidst chaos.

The days leading up to Sunday were particularly challenging for Afolabi. The plaster on his little finger significantly slowed his typing speed, transforming his usually fluid movements into a frustrating dance of clumsy keystrokes. In any other situation, he would have torn it off without a second thought, irritated by the hindrance it caused. However, this time, he refrained, motivated by his desire to please Yetunde. He treated the bandage with care, keeping it as clean and dry as possible, as if its very presence were a token of their brief yet meaningful connection.

With each passing day, Afolabi's anticipation for the Sunday fellowship grew stronger—not just for the opportunity to worship but also for the chance to see Yetunde again. He found himself lost in daydreams of their conversation, replaying the concern in her eyes and the softness of her touch. The memory lingered with him, stirring a spark of hope and excitement that overshadowed the frustration of his injury.

"Brother Afolabi," Yetunde called, startling him as he was absorbed in his computer screen. He was responsible for the media department of the fellowship and had been finalising the recordings from that day's service. At that moment, the anxious anticipation of her arrival faded, and he found himself lost in the rhythm of his work, his focus sharp on the task at hand.

Noticing his excitement, Yetunde smiled knowingly, a hint of amusement dancing in her eyes as she took a step back. "Never mind," she said reassuringly, her voice softening the moment. "Take your time; I'll wait for you." With that, she moved to a nearby chair, pulled out a book she had just borrowed from the fellowship library—*God's Generals*—and buried herself in its pages.

"I hope I didn't keep you waiting for too long?" Afolabi asked apologetically.

"Not at all," Yetunde replied with a warm smile. "By the way, how's your little finger doing?"

"Oh, that?" He shrugged, narrowing his large eyes into two crescents as he grinned. "I feel little to no pain there anymore."

"Let me take a look, as that's the main reason I decided to stay back."

Afolabi eagerly extended his hand to her, a flicker of anticipation rushing through him.

"It's healed. You don't need this anymore." With a gentle touch, she peeled away the plaster, revealing his little finger; which was now almost completely healed and free of any signs of injury.

They chatted comfortably for a while longer, the conversation flowing effortlessly, filled with laughter and shared stories, until Yetunde stood up to leave.

"Wow! We've spent quite a bit of time together without realising it." She glanced at her phone repeatedly, surprise etched across her face.

"I should be leaving now," she added, although her tone revealed a hint of reluctance.

"Let me see you off," Afolabi offered, a hopeful glint in his eyes.

"But before we leave, would you mind giving me your phone number?"

"No, I don't. Let me have your phone," Yetunde said with a playful smile. As Afolabi handed it to her, she deftly entered her number, her fingers dancing across the screen with ease before returning the phone to the elated Afolabi.

"Here you go! Now you have no excuse not to call," she teased, a glimmer of mischief in her eyes. As Afolabi and Yetunde neared the gate, the sight of the security officers stationed at the entrance reminded him of the rules he had forgotten—the strict visiting hours. The excitement he had felt just moments earlier now faded, replaced by a quiet sense of disappointment. His steps slowed, and the distance between them seemed to stretch longer than it should have.

He glanced at Yetunde, offering a smile that didn't quite reach his eyes. "I suppose this is where we part ways," he said, his voice soft but resigned.

Yetunde tilted her head slightly, her gaze softening with understanding. "It's just the rules, Afolabi. You know how strict they are here."

Afolabi sighed and ran a hand through his hair, frustration bubbling inside. "I know. I just... I just wanted more time. To walk you to your room and for us to talk a little longer. I guess I'm not quite ready for this to end."

Yetunde gave a slight, reassuring nod. "We'll see each other again soon. Fellowship on Sunday, remember? It's not the end, just a little pause."

He nodded slowly, his heart settling a bit as he remembered that their friendship, founded on their shared faith, would continue to grow in God's timing. "Take care," he said, his voice calm but sincere.

"I will," Yetunde replied, her words firm with the quiet assurance that they would both continue to walk in faith, no matter the distance between them.

Afolabi stood there for a moment, watching her walk through the gate, his heart heavy but anchored in a mix of admiration and longing. He didn't move until she disappeared around the corner, the space between them growing as if it were meant to keep him at a distance, though neither of them had asked for it.

With a deep breath, Afolabi turned and walked back towards the university's main gate. The quiet evening enveloped him, the soft rustle of leaves and the distant hum of students heading to their hostels accompanying his steps. Although a sense of disappointment still lingered, he found some comfort in the thought of seeing Yetunde again soon. The warmth of their connection, the ease of their conversations, and the way her presence always seemed to calm him—these memories lifted his spirits as he made his way to his apartment.

Afolabi and Yetunde's friendship grew slowly and steadily as they spent more time together after fellowship. They began to stay after the service, reflecting on the day's message and debating it in the chapel's quiet corners. What started as casual discussions about shared reflections quickly evolved into something more—a ritual. It was a time for them to connect both spiritually and emotionally. Afolabi had come to look forward to these moments when the world's clamour would fade away, allowing them to talk about their lives, dreams, and faith. It wasn't long before their conversations extended beyond the confines of the chapel.

At the end of the fellowship, Afolabi would escort Yetunde to her hostel, a simple act that had become a quiet tradition between them. It wasn't anything extraordinary, but for Afolabi, it symbolised the growing trust and camaraderie they had developed over time. He saw Yetunde not just as a fellow believer but as a confidant, someone with whom he could talk without fear of judgment. He was always mindful of her boundaries, ensuring that he respected her space. Yet, there was an unspoken understanding between them; their friendship was rooted in trust, free from expectations, and built on the shared comfort of each other's company.

The walk was always peaceful, filled with easy conversation and moments of silence that felt natural rather than awkward. The sort of silence that only true friends could share.

In the weeks that followed, Yetunde began visiting Afolabi's house off campus, often accompanied by a friend. It turned out to be the same lady who had helped him the day he tripped and fell, which was a delightful surprise for both. Occasionally, Yetunde would come alone, but she always made sure her boundaries were clear and respected. Her visits were a delight; she would prepare delicious meals for him, showcasing both her culinary talent and her care.

The aroma of her cooking would fill the humble flat, creating a comforting atmosphere that Afolabi had grown to appreciate. It was during these moments, enveloped by her cooking skills and the warmth of her company, that Afolabi truly began to understand the depth of her character. He felt a growing sense of responsibility and vowed to do his best to make her happy, trusting that God would guide him. Furthermore, he became determined to live up to the wisdom in Proverbs Chapter 20, verse 6B, which asks, "...but a faithful man, who can find?" This verse became his personal mantra, a constant reminder to stay true to his faith and integrity. With sharpened focus, every step he took from that point forward was intentional, driven by a deep desire to be the kind of man she could depend on.

As their friendship deepened, Afolabi found himself increasingly attracted to Yetunde's steadfast faith, her kindness, and the way she managed the demands of her life with such quiet grace. He admired her ability to uphold her values, even when faced with challenges, and he respected the boundaries she set—never once allowing his growing feelings to cloud his judgement.

Afolabi had always been financially independent, a trait that set him apart from his peers. Since gaining admission to the University of Ibadan, his IT expertise has opened doors to numerous freelance projects, providing him with a steady income. His skills were in demand, and his reputation grew with each project he undertook. This financial independence gave him a sense of pride and stability, allowing him to support himself throughout his studies without relying on his parents.

It also instilled the confidence to begin planning his future. So, as soon as he graduated, he commenced the process of his marriage to Yetunde, finding no reason anyone should question his decision.

Their relationship, which had flourished through moments of shared faith, friendship, and mutual respect, was something he cherished deeply. He knew that Yetunde was the one with whom he wanted to build his life. In his mind, the financial independence he had worked so hard to attain was the foundation for the life he envisioned creating with Yetunde—a life built on respect, value, love, trust, and shared dreams.

Shortly after returning to Lagos, he secured a reasonably well-paying job, further solidifying his sense of stability and independence. This was more than just a job; it was a testament to his hard work and dedication throughout his studies.

With this newfound financial security, Afolabi felt a renewed sense of purpose. Determined to carve his own path, he secured modest accommodation in Bariga, Lagos, opting not to stay with his parents. This decision marked a significant step in his journey—one that allowed him to fully embrace adulthood while preparing for a future with Yetunde. He relished the thought of building a home of his own, however small, and envisioned a life filled with shared dreams and aspirations.

Living in Bariga allowed him to forge his identity outside of his family. He furnished the flat with the essentials—simple furnishings and small touches that reflected his personality. Each item he selected symbolised his independence and the life he aspired to create.

Nine months after their wedding, Yetunde graduated as a nurse, a significant milestone that marked the culmination of years of hard work and dedication. Her graduation was not only a personal achievement but also a testament to her resilience and commitment to her profession. She joined Afolabi in Lagos, bringing with her a renewed sense of purpose and determination.

Soon after settling back into their home, Yetunde secured a position at a nearby private hospital. The job provided her with a sense of fulfilment and excitement, allowing her to apply her skills in a practical setting while also giving her the opportunity to contribute to their household income. Her new role as a nurse not only complemented Afolabi's work but also reinforced their shared vision for a bright future.

As they navigated the early stages of married life, their love blossomed, strengthened by shared experiences and mutual support. They celebrated each other's successes, encouraged one another during challenging moments, and cultivated a warm, loving home together. They became each other's cheerleaders, offering words of encouragement and firm belief in one another's potential.

In the evenings, after long days at work, they would sit together over shared meals, recalling the day's activities while exchanging playful banter and sharing stories that reminded them of their journey together. Small gestures of affection—a gentle touch, a warm smile, or a simple "I love you"—became the threads that wove their lives together, nurturing their bond as a young couple.

As they continued to nurture their relationship, Afolabi and Yetunde learned to embrace both the joys and struggles that came their way. They realised that love wasn't just about the good times but also about standing together through adversity, finding hope in each other, and building a future together. With each passing day, their love deepened, serving as an anchor in the stormy seas of life in Lagos.

The harsh economic realities of Nigeria were impossible to ignore, serving as a constant reminder of the challenges that loomed over their lives. Every day, they confronted the weight of struggle—a persistent presence that shaped their existence in both visible and subtle ways. The rising cost of living added a burden that pressed down on their spirits. Each month brought new obstacles: soaring prices for basic necessities, limited job opportunities, and the daily stress of making ends meet. Every step forward felt marked by the tension between their hopes and the practical barriers that appeared to hinder them. Yet, through it all, their bond remained a source of strength. In the midst of these trials, they found solace in their faith, trusting that God's provision would see them through.

With a fierce determination, they began to devise a plan for their escape. The idea of moving abroad had once seemed like a distant dream, but the more they faced the reality of their situation, the more it became a tangible goal. They spent countless evenings discussing their aspirations, weighing the pros and cons, and researching potential countries where they could seek better opportunities. Together, they committed to making it happen, trusting that their hard work and God's guidance would lead them toward a brighter future.

"We can't continue like this," Afolabi stated one evening, his expression tense as concern settled on his face. "There has to be a way for us to provide more for ourselves and our future."

Yetunde nodded in agreement, her eyes filled with hope and resolve. "I know we can make it work. We need to find the right path for us, somewhere we can thrive and maximise our potential."

They sought advice from friends who had successfully made similar moves abroad and researched the requirements for visas and job applications.

As the months passed, their visions of a new life abroad began to form in their minds. Afolabi envisioned the possibilities of advancing his IT career, while Yetunde dreamt of expanding her nursing skills in a different healthcare environment. They were excited about the prospect of a more stable financial future and the chance to provide their unborn children with better opportunities.

With hope in their hearts and determination in their spirits, Afolabi and Yetunde began exploring the various options available to them in their quest for a better life. It was during this period of hopeful aspiration that their twins were born—a joyous event that only intensified their resolve to improve their livelihood. As they held their children in their arms, Afolabi and Yetunde knew they must create a brighter future for their family—one filled with opportunity and stability. The arrival of Dara and Dami brought immeasurable joy to their lives, igniting a fierce determination to ensure their children had access to the best education and a nurturing environment.

Yetunde looked down at the tiny faces of her lovely daughters, filled with love and gratitude. "We have to make this work, Afolabi," she said, her voice shaky with emotion. "For them. They deserve the very best."

Afolabi nodded, feeling the weight of responsibility settle squarely on his shoulders. "We will give them everything we can. We can't allow the struggles of today to define their future." His resolve hardened as he thought of the life they envisioned—a life where their children could thrive, free from the financial burdens that had shackled their own dreams.

The twins were a beacon of hope, inspiring Afolabi and Yetunde to work even harder. Their lives, filled with sleepless nights and diaper changes, also brimmed with laughter and moments of pure joy. Afolabi found himself stealing glances at Yetunde as she breastfed the girls, marvelling at her strength and dedication. He felt grateful to have her by his side, sharing not just the burdens but also the joys of parenthood.

"Imagine the adventures they'll have," Yetunde said one evening as they sat together on the living room floor, surrounded by the scattered toys of their twins. Her voice held a quiet wonder as she gazed out of the window, where the fading light of dusk cast long shadows across the room. "Traveling to new places and meeting new friends. We'll give them a chance at a world we never had."

Afolabi smiled, his heart brimming with pride. "Exactly. And we'll be there with them, guiding them every step of the way." The thought of their little family exploring new horizons filled him with hope, dispelling the shadows of doubt that sometimes clouded his mind.

However, the challenges of daily life persisted. The fatigue of parenting and the ever-looming responsibilities often felt overwhelming. Nevertheless, Afolabi and Yetunde found solace in their shared aspirations and the bond they had forged through the trials they faced together.

They created a system to manage their time more efficiently, ensuring they carved out moments for each other amidst the chaos. Whether it was a quiet cup of tea after the twins had gone to bed or simply sitting together in the living room to watch films, they treasured these small moments of connection.

As the months passed and their plans solidified, Afolabi and Yetunde felt a renewed sense of purpose. Their dream of moving abroad transformed from a distant aspiration into a tangible goal, one they were determined to achieve for the sake of their children. Together, they would overcome the obstacles in their path, driven by their love for one another and the strength of their growing family.

Chapter 2

The Move

"Afolabi, are you for real? You can't be serious! Are you crazy or something?" Bolanle's voice pierced through the phone, sharp and incredulous. Afolabi winced, pulling the mobile away from his ear for a moment before pressing it back, trying to steady himself.

"Wait, you mean you want to make a woman you just met and married barely three years ago the main applicant? Have you completely lost your senses or something?" she demanded.

Afolabi sighed as he paced back and forth in the modest living room in Bariga, Lagos. Meanwhile, he kept glancing at the gate in anticipation of Yetunde's return from where she had gone to grind pepper for stew, knowing he needed to conclude this conversation before she came back.

"Sister mi," Afolabi called respectfully in his usual manner when addressing his elder sister, "you need to calm down. It's not what you think." He paused to gather his thoughts, trying to clarify the reasoning behind their decision. "We've really considered this thoroughly, and it is more logical for Yetunde to be the main applicant. This way, I can be the dependant. It gives me the freedom to change jobs whenever I wish, rather than being stuck in a care job for the next five years."

"Logical? Did I just hear you say logical? Oh, so you think it's logical to hand over all control to

"Yetunde? Have you not heard the stories making waves abroad? Women change when they arrive in the Western world. They become unrecognisable!" Bolanle's frank words were like daggers thrust through the speaker of the phone, stabbing deep into his heart.

"Sister, listen to me," said Afolabi, desperately trying to steady his voice. "Yetunde is not like that. We have been through a lot together. She is a born-again, fervent, and devoted Christian. I can vouch for her; nothing can ever change her."

"Things are not as you think, Afolabi. You cannot predict how a woman will behave until you place her in a position of power. I have witnessed this occur several times, even here in Canada. When some women gain a little power, they suddenly forget their husbands and families. You're putting yourself at risk, Afolabi, and I am not comfortable with such an arrangement."

Afolabi rubbed his forehead, aware of how deeply his sister's concerns weighed on her. "Sister mi, I believe in her. This is for my family. Yetunde, being the primary applicant, makes sense. Besides, she is a nurse, which gives us better chances with the visa process."

"But how about you, Afolabi? What if things didn't go well? What if..."

"No, now, that will never happen!" Afolabi interjects, his voice rising in protest as he abruptly interrupts her questions. His frustration bubbles to the surface, unwilling to entertain any more doubts. "We've made our decision, and Sister mi, you should know me better than this. If no one else does, at least you do." He paused, taking a breath to steady himself, his chest rising and falling as he struggled to regain control of his emotions.

"This isn't about distrust," he continued, his tone firm yet imploring. "It's about making the best choice for our future—our future. Yetunde is my wife. We've prayed about this and believe with all our hearts that we have made the right decision. Why not trust my judgment?" His voice softened towards the end, pleading for her understanding.

Bolanle sighed, her words laced with caution. "Afolabi, I'm not saying Yetunde isn't a good woman. But I've witnessed how relationships can shift when power dynamics change. Once a woman experiences that kind of freedom—the kind that comes with being in control, especially in a place like the United Kingdom—it can change her. Even good women change, little by little. Before you know it, they're not the same person you once thought they were. I'm just saying, don't be naive. Pay attention. Love alone isn't always enough to hold things together when power dynamics shift." She paused and added, "Trust me, I've seen it happen more times than you'd expect."

"I get that, Sister mi, honestly," Afolabi replied in a calm tone. "But you need to trust me. Trust us. We're in this together, working towards common goals for ourselves and our family." Afolabi felt a wave of defensiveness rise within him, irritated by the suggestion that Yetunde might change. He opened his mouth to argue, but Bolanle's warning lingered long after the call had ended, her words echoing in his mind. Could Yetunde truly change? Would this move test their marriage in ways he hadn't anticipated? He shook his head, trying to dispel the growing unease. Yetunde is different, he reassured himself. She wouldn't change.

That was how Bolanle reluctantly agreed to support their decision to make Yetunde the main applicant. Afolabi felt a heavy weight lift from his shoulders, as convincing his sister had given him sleepless nights. With her blessing, he experienced a renewed sense of determination; Bolanle's promise to help finance their relocation to the UK had lifted a significant financial burden from him.

It was no longer just about his dreams—he had the support of his sister, and that made all the difference. With this newfound resolve, Afolabi was more committed than ever to ensuring that this opportunity would not only work for them but also strengthen their relationship and pave the way for a brighter future.

Afolabi and Yetunde were two young individuals driven by great aspirations. For them, relocating to the United Kingdom symbolised more than just a change of scenery—it represented opportunity, a place where they could fully realise their dreams and give their daughters the chance to thrive.

The living room was bathed in a soft, golden glow from the setting sun, casting a warm, comforting light over Yetunde and Afolabi as they diligently packed their belongings into suitcases. Each item they folded and tucked away seemed to carry with it a memory, a piece of the life they had built together. The decision to relocate to the UK was momentous, signifying a fresh start in their journey, and the atmosphere was a blend of anticipation and wistfulness. The walls, once filled with sounds of laughter and everyday life, now stood as silent witnesses to the life they had shared, which would soon become a distant memory.

Yetunde meticulously folded a dress, her hands moving with quiet care as she placed it gently into one of the suitcases. The intricate patterns woven into the material caught her eye as she put it in the suitcase. Although she had worn this dress many times, she had paid little attention to its details, but now, in the stillness of the moment, the design seemed to take on new significance. The patterns flowed like memories, each stitch reminding her of moments she had experienced, the familiar comfort of home, and the life she and Afolabi had built together. A wave of nostalgia washed over her, soft yet undeniable, as the reality of their impending journey began to sink in.

"Afolabi," she called dreamily, her voice imbued with nostalgia. "Do you recall our first date?" "How could I forget?" he responded, looking up from his packing with a smile. "Such memories are evergreen. They can't be erased.

Yetunde giggled softly, her eyes twinkling with the same warmth that had drawn him in from the start. She pulled the lemon-coloured dress from the suitcase, allowing the fabric to gleam in the light.

"Does this strike a chord?" she asked playfully, holding it up for him to see.

Afolabi paused, his gaze locking onto the dress. The lemon colour seemed to glow under the bright overhead light, and in an instant, the memory of that day flooded back. His lips curved into a knowing smile.

"It does," he said, his tone softening. "That day... you wore that dress, and everything about you seemed to be enchanting."

Memories of their first date, a few weeks after their first encounter, flooded his mind. He could still recall how Yetunde appeared anxious when it was time to order food. She blushed slightly, unsure of what to order, as her eyes darted between the menu and him. Her uncertainty only made her more endearing, serving as a quiet reflection of her humility. Eventually, with a gentle smile, she mustered the courage to order jollof rice and a bottle of Coca-Cola—a simple yet elegant choice that perfectly mirrored her unassuming nature.

He fondly recalled their lengthy conversation that evening as the soft ambience of the Alliance café in Agbowo, Ibadan, illuminated her face. Every word she uttered only deepened his admiration for her. It was an evening filled with joy and meaningful connection, a night that firmly convinced Afolabi that Yetunde was truly extraordinary.

Afolabi paused in his packing, his expression softening. A grin spread across his lips as he looked at her, his eyes gleaming with nostalgia. "How on earth did that slip my mind?" he mused, shaking his head with a playful chuckle. "You were wearing that breathtaking blue dress, confidently ordering jollof rice like it was your signature dish." His grin widened as the memory unfolded. "We ended up talking for hours, so engrossed in our conversation that we didn't even notice the time. The restaurant practically had to kick us out."

Yetunde laughed, her eyes sparkling with delight as the memory washed over her. "Yes, we were both so anxious, stumbling over our words like nervous schoolchildren," she recalled, a teasing smile spreading across her face. "I remember you persistently asking if I wanted more rice, and I kept declining just to keep the conversation going. It felt like a game of verbal chess, trying to navigate our nerves while avoiding awkward silences."

Afolabi chuckled, shaking his head in admiration. "You were incredibly steadfast in your commitment to your beliefs," he said, his voice warm with appreciation. "I had never met anyone with such unshakable dedication. I still remember our conversation about the importance of prioritising friendship over traditional dating. You made me see relationships in a whole new light.

Yetunde nodded, a hint of a smile playing on her lips as she recalled her convictions. "I was quite determined, wasn't I?" she mused, her eyes glinting with the memory. "I believed that to stay true to God's path, I needed to steer clear of the potential pitfalls I perceived in worldly relationships. I was convinced that anything less than complete dedication was utterly unacceptable."

Her voice softened as she continued, the weight of her beliefs evident in her expression. "It was important to me to build a foundation based on faith and friendship rather than merely adhering to societal norms."

Afolabi's smile widened as he gently took her hand. "You were," he said softly, his eyes filled with admiration. "And I admired that about you. You helped me understand that our connection needed to be built on something much deeper than the physical attraction."

His voice softened, carrying the weight of the revelation that had shaped their bond. "You showed me that real love—lasting love—comes from shared values and a commitment that transcends the surface."

Yetunde gently squeezing his hand, her gaze locked with his, filled with sincerity. "It was challenging in the beginning," she admitted, her voice soft but steady. "I remember when you suggested spending more time together, and I firmly insisted on maintaining boundaries. It wasn't because I didn't care for you—quite the opposite. I cared for you deeply. But I believed that keeping those boundaries was essential to upholding our faith."

Afolabi's eyes sparkled with admiration, his smile reflecting his profound respect for her tireless commitment. "And you were right," he said in a warm voice. "Those boundaries enabled us to cultivate a stronger bond. It wasn't always easy, but the journey drew us closer. Ultimately, the challenges fortified our connection. It was worth every moment."

Yetunde smiled, her eyes softening as they drifted to a distant memory. There was something about the way his features softened in the light, the strength of his jawline and the quiet intensity of his gaze that always made her feel grounded and safe, as if nothing could shake their bond. She remembered that evening after campus fellowship when he walked her back to Idia Hall. She couldn't help but notice how naturally handsome he looked—his broad shoulders and the way his eyes sparkled when he spoke, as though the world itself was unfolding before him.

"I remember that evening after campus fellowship when you walked me back to Idia Hall," she said softly, her voice warm with nostalgia. "We talked about your aspirations and your vision for the future. I was struck by how passionately you spoke, not just about your goals but also about your deep commitment to our shared beliefs. Your dedication to both your dreams and our faith left a lasting impression on me." She smiled, her words a gentle tribute to the man he was—inside and out.

"That night was a turning point for me," Afolabi confessed, his voice thick with emotion. "It was at that moment I realised that what we shared was far more than a fleeting connection. You showed me the importance of patience and truly respecting the journey we were on together. Your genuine commitment made me see relationships in a different light—one built on trust, faith, and mutual respect."

They stood in silence for a moment, hands intertwined, both lost in the vivid memories of their journey together. The room was filled with a quiet understanding, a testament to the years of love and faith they had built. Afolabi finally broke the silence, his voice brimming with hope and quiet determination. "This move to the UK will be a fresh start for us," he said softly. "It's a chance to build on everything we've already achieved, to grow even stronger together, and to deepen the bond we share. I know we can make this work."

Yetunde nodded, her eyes glowing with firm resolve. "Indeed, it is," she said, her voice steady yet filled with warmth. "We'll continue building our lives on the same core values that brought us together—faith, respect, and love. Those are the foundations that will guide us regardless of where this journey leads us."

Afolabi gently wrapped his arms around her, pulling her into a tender embrace. "I couldn't have asked for a more perfect friend, partner, wife, and mother to our children," he whispered, his voice thick with emotion. "No matter what challenges come our way, we'll face them together— stronger and united.

With you by my side, I know we'll reach our goals."

Yetunde leaned against him, a wave of emotions swelling in her chest as she savoured the warmth of his embrace. "I feel the same way," she whispered, her voice soft yet firm with conviction. "I'm excited to begin this new journey with you, and I can't wait to see where it takes us."

He recalled a strong feeling of pride and satisfaction as he reflected on Yetunde. She embodied all the qualities he had always desired in a wife- a refined upbringing, a deep reverence for God, and a profound sense of empathy that touched everyone around her. In every aspect, she was an exceptional wife, nurturing, supportive, and inspiring. Her presence in his life constantly reminded him how fortunate he was, and he felt grateful for the love they shared.

"So, how could Sister mi conceive such a strange idea? How could she possibly think that someone as wonderful as Yetunde would betray me?" Afolabi's heart raced with concern at the troubling thought. "Could it be that Sister Mi's financial support has given her the impression that she has the authority to impose her conditions on me and meddle in our relationship? No, no, no," he thought firmly, shaking his head as if to dispel the notion.

The depth of his connection with Yetunde and the authenticity of her character could not be easily undermined. He remained resolute in his belief in the love they had built together, refusing to allow others' doubts to infiltrate his heart. Their bond was strong, fortified by shared experiences and steadfast faith, and he knew that nothing could shake its foundation.

Bolanle sat comfortably in the living room of her flat in Ontario, Canada, as the soft afternoon light filtered gently through the curtains, casting a warm glow across the space. Taking a deep breath, she picked up her mobile phone and scrolled through the messages her brother had sent earlier before calling Pastor Allen, a well-known Nigerian pastor in the UK who managed a care home.

As the phone rang, she felt tension rise within her. Unable to shake her unease, she wondered how the conversation would unfold once it connected. After a few rings, Pastor Allen's warm voice greeted her, instantly easing her discomfort.

"Hello, Pastor Allen." "May the Lord bless you, sir; this is Bolanle," she began, trying to maintain a composed tone despite the anxious flutter in her stomach. "How are you, sir?" "Hello, Bolanle! It's a pleasure to hear from you." His genuine warmth radiated through the line, reminding her of the strong community they shared, even from across the ocean. She could hear faint sounds of laughter in the background—likely the residents at the care home—contributing to the sense of connection.

"I'm calling about the Certificate of Sponsorship (COS) slot that my younger brother, Afolabi, and his wife discussed with you last week," Bolanle explained, her voice steady yet imbued with determination. She took a deep breath, fully aware of its significance.

"I will be financing their relocation to the UK and was informed that you have an available slot at your care facility."

"Yes, we do have available slots for the COS," Pastor Allen confirmed, his tone professional yet warm. "However, I must inform you that the charge for a COS slot is now £20,000."

Bolanle was filled with surprise—hope intertwined with apprehension. The task ahead was substantial, but she was resolute about doing whatever it took to help her brother and his family start a new life abroad.

"Wow, that's a huge sum," she said, her voice tinged with disbelief. "The price is quite high." Pastor Allen's tone softened as he offered reassurance. "I understand your concern, Bolanle. The fee reflects the administrative costs involved, and it's become highly competitive, especially now that everyone wants to Japa!" He paused for a moment before adding, "However, if you have any concerns or questions, I'm more than happy to discuss them further."

"Thank you, Pastor Allen," Bolanle said, a ray of hope shining through her words. "Can we discuss the price further? Given the situation, I want to ensure we reach the most favourable agreement." Pastor Allen paused, his expression softening as he considered her words. "I understand where you're coming from," he said thoughtfully. "Let's see what we can do. How about we lower the fee to £15,000? That's a considerable discount, and I believe it should make things easier for you." His tone reflected a genuine effort to find a solution that would ease her burdens.

Bolanle was relieved by the lower cost. "That seems more reasonable," she said, thanking the pastor for his kindness.

"Could you please provide me with the bank details?" She asked.

"Certainly," Pastor Allen replied. "I will provide you with the necessary information to make the payment through a third-party account. Please ensure that the transaction is completed promptly, as many people are willing to pay more than what I have just charged you."

"I learned that the main applicant is a qualified nurse in Nigeria, which will significantly boost their chances of obtaining a visa; her experience would be invaluable to our care home as well," he concluded, his tone reflecting confidence in their decision.

"Yes, Pastor," Bolanle replied, feeling a surge of determination. "Once I have the necessary information, I will promptly process the payment. I truly appreciate your help in making this happen."

"No problem at all," Pastor Allen replied, his tone reassuring. "Once we receive the payment, we'll move forward with the COS application and keep you updated. You won't be left in the dark."

After ending the call, Bolanle sank back into her chair, her thoughts swirling with conflicting emotions. The negotiations had been intense, and while she felt a wave of relief at securing a reduced price for the COS slot, unease lingered in the back of her mind. She could not shake the nagging doubt about Afolabi's decision to have Yetunde as the main applicant. Would this choice truly serve their best interests, or would it complicate matters in ways she hadn't considered anticipated?"

She found herself wondering aloud why Afolabi was so insistent on Yetunde being the main applicant. "It seems like an unusual decision," she mused, her eyes narrowed in concern.

"Especially considering the expenses involved with the COS and visa application fees for all four of them, not to mention the cost of tickets." The weight of the financial burden pressed heavily on her mind, amplifying her worries about their plans.

"Is he just being overly optimistic, or is there something he's withholding from me?" Bolanle pondered, a sense of unease creeping in. "It's curious, and I can't help but wonder if there's a hidden motive behind his determination. Could it be that his excessive emphasis on Yetunde's nursing background is clouding his judgment? Or is there another factor influencing his perspective?" The questions swirled in her mind, each one adding to her apprehension about the decisions being made. Bolanle considered the broader perspective, reflecting on the possible complexities and risks at hand. "I just hope this choice doesn't lead to negative consequences down the line," Bolanle pondered. "It's a substantial amount of money, and there are numerous risks and uncertainties to consider. I need to exercise caution, despite Afolabi's confidence in Yetunde's role. We certainly don't want to encounter any further obstacles from a decision made without careful consideration."

The weight of responsibility bore heavily on her shoulders, and she resolved to keep a close eye on the unfolding situation.

The money was transferred into the account provided by Pastor Allen. As the payment went through, Bolanle clung to the hope that her brother's trust in Yetunde would be justified despite her own lingering doubts.

One evening, after weeks of careful planning and exciting conversations, Afolabi and Yetunde finally decided it was time to visit his parents in Ikeja. The weight of the evening hung heavily between them. This was not just a casual visit—it was the moment they had been dreading and anticipating in equal measure.

The warm, inviting atmosphere of the house was filled with the comforting aroma of home-cooked food, and laughter echoed around the table. As the evening progressed and the plates were tidied up by the housemaid, Afolabi could not help but feel a familiar sense of nervous excitement. The topic they had been discussing privately for weeks—the decision that would shape their future—now consumed his thoughts. With a quick glance at Yetunde, who gave him an encouraging nod, he knew it was time to bring it up topic.

Afolabi cleared his throat and leaned slightly forward. "Dad, Mum," he began, his voice firm yet infused with sentiment, "there's something important we'd like to share with you." He felt the anticipation in the air, a blend of excitement and nerves coursing through him as he prepared to share their hopes and dreams for the future.

Mr Agboola glanced up from his newspaper, his expression suddenly filled with curiosity, as if caught off guard by something unexpected. He set the newspaper aside, eager to hear what his son had to say. Meanwhile, Mrs. Agboola's gaze softened with warm attentiveness, her expression filled with maternal pride as she focused completely on Afolabi and Yetunde. The love and support in her eyes created an inviting atmosphere, encouraging them to share their news with confidence.

Afolabi drew in a steady breath, feeling the gentle warmth of Yetunde's hand resting on his beneath the table. The reassuring touch gave him the strength he needed as he prepared to speak. "Yetunde and I have been discussing our future, and want to share it with you." He hesitated for a moment, carefully selecting his words. "We're considering moving to the UK."

A hushed silence enveloped the room, the weight of Afolabi's news hanging in the air like an ethereal presence, both profound and elusive. Mr. Agboola's eyebrows knitted together in contemplation as he absorbed the information, his expression shifting from curiosity to concern. Meanwhile, Mrs Agboola's face reflected a mix of shock and apprehension, her eyes wide as she processed the implications of their decision. The silence was thick with unspoken thoughts, each family member grappling with the potential impact of this bold choice.

"Mrs. Agboola was the first to break the silence, her voice gentle yet laced with concern. "The UK? That's a big step," she said, her eyes widening slightly in surprise, a trace of anxiety creeping into her tone. —What has prompted this decision, if you don't mind me asking?"

"Yetunde sensed the need for reassurance; she leaned in slightly, her posture open as she interjected, her voice calm and steady. "It's a combination of factors," she explained. "There are career opportunities in the UK that align perfectly with our professional goals. Plus, I've received an offer for a Certificate of Sponsorship along with a position." She did not mention that the role was as a care worker, choosing instead to focus on the broader potential. She paused, allowing the weight of her words to settle before continuing, her tone gentle yet firm. "We've carefully considered our options, and we're confident this decision will benefit both of us and our children."

Mr. Agboola's gaze softened, yet a brief flicker of uncertainty lingered in his eyes, as if he were still processing the news. "Oh, I understand. You've clearly put a lot of thought into this," he said, his voice steady but tinged with emotion. "It's just... we will miss you both dearly. Lagos has always been my sanctuary." He paused to gather his thoughts, then added, "and… I mean, the rubber stamp is always there; you can always use it."

Afolabi, still lost in his own thoughts, nodded, and continued without acknowledging his father's sarcasm. "We'll miss you too, more than words can express. However, we are optimistic that this decision will provide us with opportunities for growth that were not available to us in Nigeria. We should seize these opportunities while we still have the chance." His gaze briefly flickered towards his father, trying to catch the sarcasm in the old man's tone.

"Exactly! Bee ni, bee ni, regardless of the old couple."

"I don't understand, Dad." Afolabi sat up straight in the chair and looked at his father, who returned his gaze. He couldn't read his eyes, obscured by his thick gold-rimmed glasses that reflected the light room.

"How will you not understand when you're no longer a baby?" the old man muttered, leaning his head back against the rest, his eyes narrowing with a mix of exasperation and amusement. "So, you're absolutely right," he added, his voice softening almost imperceptibly as if conceding a point, he had not fully grasped until now.

"Dad, you're just making me more confused." Afolabi fiddled with his car keys nervously.

"How fruitful a lone palm tree in the wilderness is. How great the shadow it casts! The weary look forward to it." The old man continued without shifting his gaze from his son. He completely ignored the two women who were busy with their own thing.

"Where … Where did I get it wrong, Dad?" He stammered out his question and waited.

"Where did you get it wrong?"

"Yes, Dad."

"Do you want to hear?"

"Yes, Dad. If not, I wouldn't ask."

"Now listen, I have just the two of you and one of you; I mean, your elder sister left for Canada, and I wonder if there are yet traces of coming back in her brain. At least, in her own case, she had my blessing. Now, you came here this evening to slap me. That's how my only son, my first son and heir to my empire, chose to treat his father."

Afolabi's eyes grew cloudy with unshed tears as he imagined the loneliness his father must be feeling—and would feel even more deeply upon his departure. The thought of leaving his father behind, a man who had always been a steadfast presence in his life, weighed heavily on his heart. He could see the quiet moments of solitude that lay ahead for his father, and the pain of that realisation made his throat tighten.

"I can explain, Dad."

"That you can do without us or … Does my, I mean our opinion count?" he asked, his voice tinged with a mix of hurt and confusion.

When Afolabi realised he was getting nowhere with words, he went down on his knees before his father. "I am very sorry, Dad. Ema binu si mi," he said earnestly, prostrating himself as a sign of respect and regret. The gesture reflected his deep desire to mend the rift between them and conveyed how much he valued his father's feelings.

Mrs. Agboola's eyes shimmered with unshed tears as she reached out to Yetunde, enveloping her in a profoundly emotional embrace. "Oh, my dear, it's not that we aren't happy for you. We only wish for the best for you both, and it's hard to witness your departure."

Yetunde embraced her tightly, her emotions bubbling to the surface as she spoke. "I understand, Mummy," she replied softly, feeling the warmth of her mother-in-law's love. "We'll do our best to visit as frequently as possible. This is a significant milestone for us, and we're approaching it with immense determination and optimism."

Mr. Agboola nodded slowly, his expression shifting from surprise to reluctant acceptance. "Well, if this is what you both truly believe is the right course of action, then we will support you," he said, his voice steady but tinged with concern. "Just promise me that you'll look out for one another. Family is everything, and I want to know you'll take care of each other out there."

Afolabi felt a surge of relief and was so happy. "Sure thing, Dad." Yes, we will. And we'll make sure to provide you with all the latest updates. Here's another chapter of our lives, and we'd love for you to join us on this journey".

As the evening drew to a close, the family shared more stories and laughter, the initial shock of the news fading into a sense of approval and encouragement. The path ahead promised to be filled with challenges, yet Afolabi and Yetunde found comfort in the steadfast backing and affection of their loved ones. They stood ready to embark on the exciting adventures that awaited them in the United Kingdom.

Chapter 3

A New Beginning

Two months after Afolabi visited his parents, the couple bid farewell to their neighbours in Bariga, emotions running high as they made their way to Murtala Muhammed Airport in Ikeja, Lagos. As they boarded the plane, ready for their fresh start, they exchanged a glance filled with resolve and optimism. The future stretched before them, uncertain yet full of potential, and Afolabi's family stood steadfastly by his side, embodying an unflinching commitment to one another. They were prepared to face whatever challenges lay ahead, united in their journey and strengthened by their shared dreams.

As the plane soared higher into the night sky, the vibrant lights of Lagos slowly receded beneath them, twinkling like distant memories. Afolabi and Yetunde settled into their seats, the steady hum of the engines and the gentle quivering of the aircraft creating a calming backdrop for their thoughts. The reality of their move to the UK began to sink in, a mix of excitement and uncertainty swirling within them. Along with it came a profound sense of gratitude for Bolanle's immense support—without her help, this dream might have remained out of reach.

Yetunde settled into her seat, carefully fastening her seatbelt before stealing a glance at Afolabi. Her eyes sparkled softly in the glow of the cabin lights. "I'm still in awe of what Sister Bolanle did for us," she whispered, her voice barely audible and filled with emotion. "It all feels so surreal, like I'm living in a dream."

Afolabi nodded, his eyes fixed on the seatback in front of him as he absorbed the weight of their journey. "I understand," he murmured, his voice low and reflective. "It's overwhelming, to be honest. She's always been there for me, but this... this is on a completely different level." He paused, his thoughts swirled with gratitude and disbelief. "Her support has made all the difference."

Yetunde reached out and gently took his hand—strong and rough, more like that of a boxer—squeezing it with tenderness. Her fingers delicately traced the veins on his hand as she spoke softly. "I've been thinking about how best to express my gratitude to her," she murmured, her voice full of emotion. "It's not just about the money. It's about her belief in us and our future. She's helped us turn our dreams into reality, and I want her to understand how much that means to me truly."

Afolabi glanced at her, his expression thoughtful. "I've been thinking about the same thing," he said softly. "It's more than just financial support. It's her trust in us, her constant encouragement to take this daring leap." He paused, his gaze softening as he continued, "I want to ensure she truly understands how grateful we are—for her belief in us, for all the sacrifices she's made to help us get here."

Yetunde gazed out of the window, mesmerised by how the sky darkened and the first twinkling stars appeared in the vast expanse. "Once we've found our footing, I think it would be wise to reach out to her," she said thoughtfully, her eyes still fixed on the stars. "It would mean so much to express our gratitude in person. Perhaps we could plan a visit to her in Canada, accompanied by a thoughtful gift—something that shows her how deeply we appreciate all she's done for us."

Afolabi grinned, nodding in agreement. "That sounds perfect," he said warmly. "I've already started drafting a heartfelt thank-you message, but I believe it could use a more personal touch. I want to ensure she truly understands the depth of her support—not just in practical terms, but also how much it means to us emotionally. She's been more than a helping hand; she's been a pillar for us throughout this entire journey."

"I have something I'd like to add as well," she said softly, her voice trembling slightly with emotion. "I want her to understand that this move is about so much more than just a career opportunity. It's a chance for us to grow and pursue our dreams—and it's all thanks to her belief in us. Without her support, none of this would have been possible."

Afolabi leaned closer, his voice calm yet brimming with affection. "Let's work together on our messages," he suggested, a soft smile playing on his lips. "We can each express our gratitude in our own unique ways and then combine our thoughts into one heartfelt message. That way, she'll feel the love and appreciation from both of us."

Yetunde smiled, her eyes sparkling with joy. "Sure, let's go ahead with that."

As the plane continued its journey, passengers settled into their seats, preparing for the long flight ahead. Afolabi and Yetunde, wrapped in their own intimate world of gratitude and anticipation, understood that this moment marked the beginning of a new chapter in their lives. The path ahead was filled with uncertainty, but the steady foundation of Bolanle's support had made it all possible. With hearts full of hope, they embraced the promise of what lay ahead, knowing that this transition would shape their future in ways they had only dreamed of.

They exchanged a determined and hopeful glance, their hearts brimming with gratitude for Bolanle. With every mile they soared through the sky, they carried with them a profound sense of love and belief that had fueled their remarkable journey. As they delved into discussions about their future in London, the prospect of a fresh start grew even more promising, buoyed by the comforting presence of their loved ones who would guide them along the way. Together, they felt ready to embrace the adventures and challenges that lay ahead, confident in the support that surrounded them.

Afolabi and Yetunde arrived in the UK on a cool autumn morning, the crisp air providing a refreshing change from the muggy heat they had endured in Lagos. As they stepped off the plane at Gatwick North Terminal and onto the tarmac, they were immediately greeted by the briskness of the English weather, both invigorating and unfamiliar. They had traded the lively, bustling streets of Lagos for London's more subdued and often overcast atmosphere.

The flat they had rented was simple yet tidy, nestled in Romford within a peaceful environment not far from the shopping mall and a short distance from Queen's Hospital in East London. It stood in stark contrast to their expansive home back in Nigeria, but it was theirs—a new beginning. With hope and determination, they embarked on this fresh start, aware that it would come with its fair share of obstacles, yet eager to face whatever challenges lay ahead together.

As Yetunde unpacked their belongings, she glanced at Afolabi, who was inspecting the modest, empty kitchen. The space felt cramped, and the unfamiliar layout was almost disorienting. Memories of their spacious, comfortable home in Lagos flooded her mind, starkly contrasting with the functional yet limited setting they now found themselves in. While the kitchen lacked the warmth of their previous home, it held the promise of new beginnings. She reminded herself that they would fill it with their own memories and love.

"Afolabi, have you noticed the significant drop in temperature?" Yetunde exclaimed, a shiver running down her spine as she struggled to free a winter coat from the depths of the suitcase. The chill in the air was a stark reminder that they were no longer in the warm embrace of Lagos, and she quickly wrapped the coat around her shoulders, seeking comfort from the briskness that enveloped her.

"Yes," Afolabi replied with a slight grin, trying to inject warmth into the moment as he rubbed his hands together briskly. "And I heard the temperature is expected to drop even further tonight. Honestly, I'm not sure I'm ready for this constant coldness." He chuckled lightly, attempting to mask his apprehension, but the chill in the air was a stark reminder of the adjustment they faced in their new life.

Yetunde nodded, deep in thought. "The weather in Lagos is so different from this," she mused, her voice reflecting a blend of curiosity and concern. "I'm really curious about how we'll navigate the winter. I've heard it can be quite challenging here." She wrapped her arms around herself as if to ward off the chill that lingered in the air, already contemplating the adjustments they would need to make.

"We'll adapt," Afolabi said, trying to convey a sense of optimism. "Isn't this just a thrilling part of the journey?" He paused for a moment, his expression softening. "But I must confess, I already find myself longing for the comforting embrace of home." The weight of his words lingered in the air, reminding everyone of the mixed emotions accompanying their new adventure.

They exchanged a meaningful glance, one that conveyed much about their shared determination. In that fleeting moment, they reaffirmed their resolve. Despite the challenging circumstances ahead, they remained steadfast in their commitment to succeed. Their unspoken bond was a source of strength, reassuring them that they could face any obstacle together.

The cultural differences were striking, and their initial trip to the ALDI store in Romford felt overwhelming. Yetunde pushed the twin buggy through the aisles, scowling as she navigated the vast array of products and unfamiliar brands. The multitude of options was both thrilling and bewildering. Meanwhile, Afolabi stood before a shelf brimming with an extensive selection of tea, each box boasting its unique label and flavour, leaving him equally stunned.

"This is the part where we're supposed to adapt," Yetunde remarked, lifting a packet of biscuits with a confounded expression. "I never imagined buying biscuits would turn out to be this complicated!" She chuckled softly, the humour of the situation lightening the moment as they both adjusted to their new environment.

Afolabi couldn't help but chuckle, feeling a slight lift in his mood. "We'll get used to it," he said with a reassuring smile. "Our British neighbours seem relatively friendly, at least from what I can tell. I hope their reserved demeanour doesn't come across as unwelcoming." He glanced around the store, hoping to catch a glimpse of the community they would soon be part of, eager to embrace this new chapter together.

"Based on what I've heard," Yetunde replied, her gaze thoughtfully sweeping across the shelves, "the British are known for their politeness and their tendency to keep to themselves. It might take some time for us to adjust to their ways." She paused, considering the cultural nuances they would need to navigate, her expression reflecting both curiosity and intrigue.

As the weeks passed, Yetunde seamlessly adapted to her new role at the care home. Her dedication and genuine compassion earned admiration from both her colleagues and the residents. Despite the job's challenges, including long hours and emotional strain, it provided her with a deep sense of purpose and fulfillment. Each day, she found joy in the small achievements—whether it was a smile from a resident or a heartfelt thank you from a colleague. Although the job tested her resilience, it also reaffirmed her belief in the impact of compassionate care, making each moment meaningful.

Afolabi, on the other hand, faced a unique set of challenges. Despite his impressive qualifications and extensive experience in the IT industry, he struggled to secure employment in his chosen field. The lack of UK experience loomed over him like a dark cloud, becoming a significant barrier in his job search. With each rejection email he received, he felt his confidence erode a little more, leaving him questioning his abilities and worth. The once-familiar landscape of job hunting now felt daunting, and the weight of uncertainty hung heavy on his shoulders.

One evening, as they sat in their cosy kitchen, the warm glow of the overhead light created a comforting atmosphere. The twins were blissfully engrossed in their play, their laughter filling the air and providing a soothing soundtrack to the unfamiliarity of their new circumstances. As Yetunde watched them, she felt a blend of joy and anxiety, knowing that their happiness was intricately tied to the conversations they were about to have.

"Afolabi," Yetunde began, her voice tinged with contemplation. "I've been reflecting on something. What if you consider taking a job at the care home where I work, at least for now? They're in desperate need of more hands. I know it may not align with what you want, but it could provide us with some stability while you continue searching for IT positions."

Afolabi let out a heavy sigh, his hand instinctively reaching up to run through his hair. "I didn't come all this way to work in a care home, Yetunde," he said, his tone sharp with disappointment. "It feels like a regression. I've invested so much effort into building a successful career in IT. Right now, I'm not convinced this is progression." The weight of his words hung heavily in the air, reflecting his internal struggle between ambition and the reality of their new life.

Yetunde leaned forward, her gaze steady and filled with understanding. "I empathise with how you're feeling," she said gently. "I know this may not be ideal, but it's a practical solution. With two incomes, we'll have the financial stability we need. Plus, you can continue searching for IT jobs in the meantime." Her voice was calm and reassuring, reflecting her determination to make the best of their circumstances while supporting Afolabi through his struggles.

Afolabi gazed at her, clearly impressed by her resilience. "You have a remarkable talent for making things sound more manageable," he admitted, a hint of admiration in his voice. "Alright, I'll pick it up, just for the time being." He offered a small smile, appreciating her ability to bring clarity to the situation, even as he wrestled with his own feelings about the transition.

As time passed, Afolabi became fully immersed in the daily routine at the care home. Although it was not the job he had envisioned, he found unexpected fulfilment in the strong bonds he formed with his colleagues and the rewarding nature of his tasks. The challenges he encountered were significantly different from his initial expectations; however, he gradually cultivated a profound appreciation for the sense of purpose that came with helping the elderly.

Afolabi worked the day shift while Yetunde took on a permanent night schedule, creating a balance that allowed them to fulfil their responsibilities and spend quality time with their daughters. Although this arrangement helped them save on childcare costs, the unconventional routine meant that the husband and wife spent less time together.

As Yetunde and Afolabi embraced their new life in East London, they longed for a spiritual haven that could offer the same sense of community and belonging they had cherished in Nigeria.

However, Pastor Bamidele, the pastor of the church they had attended back home in Nigeria before relocating to the UK, appeared visibly concerned when Afolabi and Yetunde shared that they had not been to church for the last two Sundays. "You must stay connected to your roots," their pastor in Nigeria advised earnestly, his voice filled with genuine care. "It's unfortunate that we are still planning to have a branch of our church in London," Pastor Bamidele remarked, his voice tinged with empathy. "Finding a place where you can feel at home in your faith is crucial, especially in a new country."

Afolabi nodded, understanding the pastor's sentiments. "After conducting a thorough search, we found that the nearest branch is in Sheffield. Unfortunately, it's over two hundred kilometres away from us, and since we aren't mobile yet, getting there will be a challenge." He sighed, the weight of their situation settling in as he reflected on the distance and limitations in this unfamiliar environment

Pastor Bamidele let out a deep sigh over the phone. "I understand, my son. Adjusting to a different environment can be quite challenging, particularly when it comes to finding a place where you feel spiritually connected. However, it's essential to prioritise your relationship with God rather than focusing solely on the distance."

His voice softened with sincerity as he continued, "More importantly, never forget your identity, no matter what happens. Remember, the greatest offering to God is a quality lifestyle of holiness and righteousness in all you do, whether in Nigeria or there in the UK. May the Lord continue to bless your home." He concluded with a heartfelt prayer, imparting a sense of comfort and strength to Afolabi and Yetunde as the call ended.

The pastor's words resonated deeply with them, offering encouragement and a renewed sense of spiritual purpose as they navigated their new life in a foreign land.

The following Sunday, Afolabi and Yetunde decided to try the church they had spotted inside the Romford Shopping Mall. As they walked in, they were immediately struck by the lively atmosphere—a welcoming energy that made them feel they had discovered something special. The setting felt just right, with songs and rhythms resonating deeply with them; the beats were unmistakably Nigerian in flavour, and the congregation's warmth and hospitality quickly put them at ease. It was precisely the kind of environment they had long yearned for, where their roots were celebrated and their spirits could connect with the music and energy around them. As they stepped into this new chapter of their lives, the joy was evident on their faces, and the meaningful glances they exchanged were filled with hope and optimism for the future.

After the service, Pastor Adewale approached the newcomers to welcome them formally. He had noticed the vibrant energy radiating from them during the praise and worship sessions and could see they were not new to the faith—there was something deeper in their expressions and posture. It was evident they were not "baby Christians" but individuals with a solid foundation in Christ, ready to contribute meaningfully to the spiritual community around them.

"Brother Afolabi, Sister Yetunde," Pastor Adewale began, his voice filled with warmth and hospitality. "It's truly a delight to have you here with us today. I can sense the excitement within you both—this marks the beginning of a new chapter brimming with endless potential. As you embark on this journey, always remember that there is a guiding presence with you. The path ahead may present its challenges—unfamiliar territory, new job opportunities, and a different way of life—but these are all integral parts of the thrilling adventure that awaits you. Every experience, every new step, shapes you for the blessings that lie ahead."

Despite its size, the church radiated warmth and hospitality, attracting a diverse congregation of Nigerians and immigrants from various African regions. It quickly became a sanctuary where individuals could find solace in their beliefs, drawing strength from familiar praise and worship songs and uplifting prayers. The welcoming atmosphere fostered a profound sense of community, providing spiritual nourishment and inspiration to all who attended.

The small, sparsely furnished flat began to feel more like home as they settled into their new routine. The following Sunday, after the church service, they decided to join a small group of Nigerians for lunch at a restaurant in South East London. The atmosphere buzzed with joyous laughter, and the delightful scent of homemade dishes filled the air. The familiar tastes and the company of fellow countrymen provided a much-needed sense of connection and belonging, reminding them of the warmth of their community back home in Nigeria. As they shared stories and laughter, the weight of their recent challenges felt lighter, and hope blossomed anew in their hearts.

"It's wonderful to see you both settling in," remarked Pastor Adewale, their new spiritual leader, as he helped himself to a generous plate of delicious yellowish-red jollof rice. "Always remember that the divine plan is designed with our best interests in mind, even if it may sometimes be hard to see."

Afolabi nodded, feeling a sense of solace in Pastor Adewale's words. "We understand, Pastor. We have faith that we are heading in the right direction." His voice conveyed a hint of determination, reflecting their shared commitment to embrace whatever challenges lay ahead.

Despite their challenges, Afolabi and Yetunde's connection deepened as they navigated their new life together. They found solace in their church community, which welcomed them with open arms. Forming new friendships and establishing connections with other Nigerians provided a comforting anchor to their cultural heritage, helping them feel less isolated in their new surroundings. Sharing meals, stories, and laughter with fellow countrymen served as a bridge to their past, nurturing their spirits and reinforcing their sense of belonging.

One evening, as they put Dara and Dami to bed, Yetunde turned to Afolabi, her eyes sparkling with gratitude and love. "I couldn't have done this without you," she said softly, her voice filled with sincerity. "We will definitely succeed; I have complete faith in us." Her words felt like a warm embrace, reminding them of their shared commitment to one another and the life they were building together, instilling a sense of hope that brightened the dim room. Afolabi enveloped her in a warm and comforting hug, feeling the weight of their shared journey in that moment. "Of course, we will, together." Their cozy flat, while simple and minimally decorated, began to feel more like a place they could truly call home. Each day was filled with fresh experiences; every obstacle they encountered only strengthened their bond.

As time passed, Afolabi and Yetunde gradually adjusted to their new life in the UK. They explored the intricacies of British culture, from the ever-changing weather to the courteous yet reserved demeanour of their neighbours. They soon realised that the British weather was just as unpredictable as its reputation, with unexpected rain showers and occasional moments of sunshine. They also experienced the British tendency for reserve, which sometimes seemed like a barrier to developing closer relationships with their new neighbours. Yet, these experiences taught them the importance of patience and perseverance in building relationships in their new environment.

The twins excelled in their nursery, immersing themselves in the local dialect and forming friendships. Observing their children thrive and grow in their new surroundings brought Afolabi and Yetunde a comforting sense of reassurance. The nursery had transformed into a familiar and welcoming space for the children, a place where they found joy and were fully engaged in learning and play. Each day brought new discoveries and laughter, affirming to Afolabi and Yetunde that their decision to relocate was not only right but also a step towards a brighter future for their family.

Nevertheless, Afolabi's search for employment continued to be a cause of great concern. He had attended numerous interviews, always hoping for a breakthrough, only to be met with polite rejections. Yetunde's encouragement and positive outlook provided him with a continual source of resilience. She reminded him of their shared aspirations and the potential for a brighter tomorrow, evoking memories of their dreams and the journey they had embarked upon together. Her belief in him served as a beacon of hope, illuminating the path ahead even in the face of adversity.

"Every setback is just a step toward success," she would say, her voice soothing and reassuring, providing comfort to his weary spirit. "We will reach our goals, Afolabi. I have absolute and unshaken faith in you." Her well-grounded belief wrapped around him like a warm embrace, rekindling his determination and reminding him that their journey was not in vain.

One day after yet another disappointing interview, Afolabi returned home feeling particularly disheartened. As he entered the kitchen, the comforting aroma of fried rice filled the air. Yetunde was engrossed in preparing dinner, and the sight of her focused efforts, along with the sound of the twins' laughter, brought him a brief moment of relief. In that instant, he was reminded of the love and warmth surrounding him, rekindling a flicker of hope in his weary heart.

"Any success today?" Yetunde inquired, her eyes sparkling with an optimistic grin that sharply contrasted with Afolabi's demeanour.

Afolabi shook his head, his shoulders drooping in resignation. "Another rejection," he replied, his voice weighed down by disappointment. "The same lame excuse — that I lack UK experience." The words lingered in the air, a stark reminder of the obstacles he faced, and he felt a familiar ache of frustration settle in his chest.

Yetunde stepped closer and wrapped her arms around him tightly. "It's unfortunate that they don't see the value in what you have to offer," she said softly, her voice filled with emotion.

"You have so much talent, and I truly believe that the perfect opportunity will come your way in due time. Until then, we'll be doing this together. We are building our life here, one step at a time." She pulled back slightly to meet his gaze, her eyes reflecting determination. "Thank God we're still managing to meet our bills with the care work we're doing."

Her words inspired him to persevere. However, he knew deep down that the care work he was doing at the time was not what he had planned. Despite the difficulties, they tackled every hurdle with determined resolve. They drew strength from their deep love and unwavering commitment to one another. Their journey was still ongoing, but with their persistent belief and the encouragement they received, they were confident in their ability to overcome any obstacles that lay ahead.

As they gathered around the dinner table, the twins animatedly chattered about their day, and Afolabi could not help but feel a surge of appreciation wash over him. Regardless of the challenges they faced, their unity was the most important thing.

"We'll make it," he assured, locking eyes with Yetunde across the table. "I assure you." She smiled, her eyes sparkling with a resolute determination. "It's just a matter of time," she replied confidently, her voice firm. The warmth of their connection filled the room, reinforcing their shared resolve to navigate the challenges ahead together.

Pastor Adewale let out a deep sigh as Afolabi narrated how difficult it was for him to find a job. His face reflected empathy as he gently placed a reassuring hand on Afolabi's shoulder. "I understand, my son. Adjusting to a new environment can be quite challenging, especially when it comes to securing your desired job. However, it's important to maintain hope in God, knowing fully that He will fulfil His plans in His own time." He looked directly into Afolabi's weary eyes and continued, "Stay steadfast in your belief, lean on one another, and rely on your community of faith here. Remember that you have a support system throughout this journey—the divine presence and our own. There are brighter days on the horizon, and when they arrive, you'll reflect on your journey and realise the progress you've made."

Afolabi nodded, feeling a newfound resolve. "I have faith in God's plan, Pastor. I believe there is a purpose behind my presence in the UK, and I will persist in my journey with unfaltering faith." He sighed heavily, instinctively smoothing his thick black eyebrows with his left index finger. "Thank you, Pastor," he said, his voice filled with gratitude. "That was exactly what I needed to hear."

As Afolabi left the church that day with his family, he was filled with a renewed sense of optimism. Their journey was still unfolding, and while obstacles loomed on the horizon, he felt a deep sense of confidence in the strength of his beliefs, his wife's steadfast support, and the church community's resilience to guide him forward.

Chapter 4

The Job

Life outside Nigeria had been challenging for the Afolabis. Afolabi had never envisioned working in the care sector. However, unforeseen circumstances beyond his control compelled him to take this uncharted path. The couple found themselves with little time for family devotions, either in the mornings or evenings. The demands of their new work schedules were taking a heavy toll on their conjugal, personal, and spiritual lives. Despite the strain, Yetunde and Afolabi continued to encourage each other to persevere, although both were beginning to feel the emotional and psychological distance growing between them. Arguments and outbursts, once rare, had become more frequent, and their attendance at fellowship gatherings had become irregular. Even their twin daughters seemed affected by the tension in the home.

"Well, returning to Nigeria is no longer an option," Afolabi murmured to himself, his voice barely above a whisper as he dragged his weary body into the house. "I hope and believe that I'll find a job that I genuinely want soon." Each word felt heavy on his tongue, a blend of determination and fatigue swirling within him. The dim light of their living room cast long shadows, mirroring the weight of his thoughts as he stepped inside, yearning for the comfort of home amidst the uncertainty.

After months of relentless job hunting and countless disappointments, Afolabi returned home late one gloomy Thursday evening, his body heavy with exhaustion from another grueling shift at the care home. The weight of fatigue seemed to settle into his bones as he sank into the worn sofa, his thoughts swirling with a mix of doubts and fleeting hopes.

Suddenly, his phone vibrated in his pocket, shattering the heavy silence of the room. A wave of tension washed over him as memories flooded back—each job rejection, every time he had answered a call from a withheld number, only to hear the words he dreaded most. The feeling of hope rising in his chest, only to be crushed under the weight of disappointment, was all too familiar.

Each missed opportunity carved a deeper sense of uncertainty within him, and the thought of facing yet another letdown unsettled him. As he stared at the phone, the unknown number felt like a double-edged sword, promising possibility yet taunting him with the risk of heartbreak. Would this call finally bring the news he longed for, or would it simply add to the growing list of frustrations that haunted his dreams?

He took a deep breath, feeling the weight of the moment. After what seemed like an eternity, he steeled himself and finally decided to answer the call, ready to face whatever news awaited him. "Hello, this is Chloe from British Telecom. May I please speak with Afolabi?"

As soon as he heard "British Telecoms," a jolt of electricity surged through him, tightening his chest. His breath caught for a moment, and he sensed the world around him narrowing, the hum of the room fading into the background. Memories of the interview played back in his mind—the hopeful anticipation mixed with a lingering fear of rejection. He could almost feel the weight of the moment pressing down, the stakes higher than ever. Afolabi's heart raced as he braced himself, aware that this call could tip the balance between despair and a new opportunity beginning.

"Hello, this is Afolabi speaking," he replied, trying to sound composed despite his fatigue.

"Good evening, Mr. Afolabi," came a warm, professional voice from the other end. "This is Chloe from BT. How are you doing?"

Afolabi's heart pounded as he struggled to find his voice. The casual question felt like a cruel distraction, pulling him deeper into the whirlwind of his thoughts. Hadn't he just poured every ounce of hope into that interview? "Uh, it's been alright," he replied, his voice steadier than he had anticipated.

"That's good to hear," Chloe continued, her tone friendly yet professional. "I wanted to reach out regarding your recent interview with us. I hope this is a good time to talk."

The mention of his interview sent a rush of heat to his cheeks, and he could almost hear his own heartbeat echoing in his ears. A brief silence hung between them, stretching like a taut wire, filled with unspoken possibilities. He could feel the weight of her next words bearing down on him, the tension thick enough to cut. Would this be the moment he had been waiting for, or another disappointment wrapped in polite conversation?

"Yes, please," Afolabi said

"Thank you. I'm pleased to inform you that

after careful consideration, we would like to offer you the position of IT Support Specialist in our " organisation."

Afolabi froze, the words not registering immediately. "I... I got the job?" he stammered, his heart racing.

"Yes, Mr. Afolabi," Chloe confirmed with a smile in her voice. "We were truly impressed with your interview, and we would be delighted to have you join us." team."

Afolabi's breath hitched in his throat, and for a moment, the world around him faded. He replayed her words, each one sinking in like a weightless feather that suddenly felt heavy with significance. "Congratulations," she had said. The finality of it resonated, stirring a mix of disbelief and joy within him. He could hardly process the reality, the months of uncertainty, the countless rejections, all leading to this moment. A smile broke across his face, but it was tinged with an edge of vulnerability. Would this truly be the fresh start he had been longing for?

"Thank you so much," Afolabi replied, his voice heavy with emotion. "You have no idea how much this means to me."

You're very welcome," Chloe said warmly. "We'll send the conditional offer letter via email, and once all the checks are completed and the references are received, your manager will get in touch with you to agree on a start date."

After ending the call, Afolabi sat in stunned silence for a moment, the weight of the moment sinking in. His heart raced as disbelief mingled with jubilation, leaving him breathless. In an instant, he leapt to his feet, a surge of adrenaline coursing through him and electrifying every nerve. He rushed to the kitchen, where Yetunde was busy preparing dinner before setting off for the night shift.

"Yetunde!" he exclaimed triumphantly, "Guess what, I got the job!"

Yetunde turned around, her eyes filled with astonishment and delight. "Wow!" She exclaimed, clearly stunned by the news. "Afolabi, are you serious?" She hurried over to him and swept him into her arms with an affectionate hug.

He nodded, a wide grin lighting up his face. "Yes, I just received the call. I'm excited to tell you that I, Afolabi Agboola, will be joining British Telecom as an IT Support Specialist!"

Yetunde's eyes brimmed with tears of joy as she held him tightly. "Oh, Afolabi, this is good news! I had a feeling this would happen to you; I just had a feeling!"

Afolabi completely enveloped her in a hug, fully realising the magnitude of his fresh start. "This means I can finally move on from my care job and dedicate myself to my true passion. "It's a fresh beginning for us, Yetunde."

"I am filled with immense pride for you," she whispered, gazing up at him with eyes sparkling with admiration. "You persevered, even in the face of adversity. This is only the beginning, Afolabi. We are going to achieve everything we have ever dreamed of."

As they joyfully celebrated the news, Afolabi politely excused himself to make some calls. First, he dialled Pastor Adewale's number. After a few rings, the call connected, and his voice came through in the usual calm and reassuring tone.

"Blessed one, how are you today?"

"Good evening, Pastor. I just wanted to share some exciting news with you. I received the job offer we've been hoping for! I couldn't wait to share this good news with you."

"That's our God for you, Brother Afolabi! He truly does incredible things!" Pastor Adewale said warmly. "There is God at work in your life!" This is just the beginning of countless blessings on the horizon. Keep trusting Him, and I am so happy for you."

After his uplifting conversation with Pastor Adewale, Afolabi reached out to Bayo, a dependable friend and mentor who had supported him since he first arrived in the UK.

"Bayo, guess what? I got the job!" Afolabi exclaimed, his voice filled with excitement. Bayo smiled from the other end. "I always believed in your abilities, Afolabi!" This is just the beginning of great things to come. I am very impressed with you, my dear friend.

You must *wash* this for me ooo; we should definitely celebrate this significant achievement soon." After Afolabi ended the call, a profound feeling of gratitude washed over him. Yetunde, Pastor Adewale, and Bayo's support made the victory even sweeter. He was confident that with their support and dedication, this next phase would bring even greater success.

The following day, Afolabi approached his manager, Ms Clarke, at the care home with a mix of anticipation and melancholy. He had come to value the work, the sense of belonging, and the daily rhythm, even if it wasn't what he had initially envisioned for his life. As he neared Ms. Clarke's office, he felt remorse, aware that his departure would surely create a vacuum.

"Come in," Ms. Clarke's voice beckoned from inside.

Afolabi entered the office, feeling a weight in his heart as he prepared to share the news. "Good morning, Ms. Clarke," he began, his voice steady despite the turmoil within him.

"Could I have a moment of your time?"

Ms. Clarke looked up, sensing the seriousness in his tone. "Of course, Afolabi. Please, take a seat," she said, gesturing towards the chair opposite her.

Ms. Clarke looked up from her paperwork, her friendly smile brightening the room. "How may I assist you today?" Her warm tone made it easier for him to approach the difficult conversation ahead. He took a deep breath, steadying himself before handing her the carefully sealed envelope containing his resignation letter. "I have received an offer for a position in the IT sector and will be leaving the care home at the end of my notice period."

Ms. Clarke's smile wavered as she accepted the envelope from his hand, carefully opening it and unfolding the letter. As she read, a wave of melancholy washed over her. "I'm genuinely happy for you, Afolabi; truly I am," she said, her voice filled with sincere emotion. "However, I must acknowledge that this is a significant setback for our team. You've been an invaluable asset to this organisation, and we are going to miss you," she continued.

Afolabi nodded, his throat tightening with emotion. "I have gained a wealth of knowledge and experience during my time here, and I sincerely appreciate the opportunity you provided me. It wasn't what I had anticipated, but it has proven to be fulfilling in its own unique way."

Ms Clarke let out a soft sigh, reclining in her chair as she regarded him with deep contemplation. "You've made a significant impact here, Afolabi. You are highly regarded by the residents, and your colleagues hold you in high esteem. It's not often that one encounters an individual as committed and empathetic as you."

"Thank you, Ms. Clarke," Afolabi whispered gently. "I really appreciate that. But this IT job is the culmination of years of hard work and dedication. I simply cannot resist the opportunity." "I fully understand," she responded, a slight grin returning to her face. "It's wonderful to see that you've rediscovered your passion and are now pursuing it. You deserve this." Her tone was warm and encouraging, the brief sadness giving way to pride in Afolabi's success.

Afolabi smiled, feeling a blend of emotions. "I'll also miss this place."

Ms. Clarke rose gracefully from her seat and extended her hand. "You've done a great job here, Afolabi, and I am confident that you will excel in your new position." Congratulations."

Afolabi extended his hand, feeling a surge of gratitude swell within him. "Thank you for everything, Ms. Clarke. I will always appreciate the support I received here." His voice was steady, yet the emotion behind his words was unmistakable, reflecting the deep appreciation he felt for the journey they had undertaken together.

As he left the office, Afolabi experienced a range of emotions—anticipation for what lay ahead, coupled with profound gratitude for the journey that brought him to this moment. He had encountered obstacles, gained new skills, and forged lasting relationships. Now, as he prepared to embark on a new venture, he realised that every step along the way had been worthwhile. Afolabi was prepared to face whatever challenges that lay ahead, supported by Yetunde, and propelled by his ambitions.

Chapter 5

The Encounter

Late one evening during her night shift at the care home, Yetunde's manager approached her with a gentle tap on the shoulder. "Yetunde, could I ask for your assistance with something?"

"Of course," Yetunde replied, putting aside her paperwork.

"I need you to pick up some groceries we're low on from ASDA," her manager requested.

Without hesitation, Yetunde nodded. She understood how important these small comforts were for the residents, especially in the late hours when reassurance and familiar routines mattered most. Grabbing her coat and the list, she set off into the cool night, determined to fulfil the task with care. As she stepped into ASDA, the store seemed less busy, illuminated by the gentle glow of fluorescent lights that created a stark contrast to the dimly lit corridors of the care home.

Yetunde, with a short list of items in hand, navigated the aisles with determination, her mind focused on completing her errand swiftly.

Yetunde moved quickly through the quiet aisles of ASDA, her thoughts preoccupied with many things-the tasks awaiting her back at the care home, the pressures of life in the UK, among others. The supermarket was nearly empty, with just a few scattered shoppers meandering through the aisles. She glanced at the list in her hand—simple items: milk, bread, tea, and a few personal care products for the resident. The thought of the resident waiting for these essentials fueled her determination.

Lost in her thoughts, Yetunde stood quietly in the queue at the till, her mind drifting back to the care home. Suddenly, a voice with a familiar Nigerian accent greeted her with a friendly tone.

"Hey, sis," he said with a warm and familiar tone. "You have such a vibrant look—are you a Nigerian?"

Yetunde's attention snapped back. She reciprocated his smile, feeling a glimmer of relief upon recognising the accent she knew so well. "Yes, I am." Hi there, my name is Yetunde.

"I'm Olakunle," he said casually as he began scanning her items. "It's a pleasure to come across fellow Nigerians in this setting. How long have you been here UK?

Their the conversation flowed smoothly as Olakunle scanned her groceries. Yetunde found comfort in sharing her experiences—the challenges of working night shifts, the constant adjustments to a foreign culture, and her aspirations for a more seamless transition. Olakunle shared his personal anecdotes and offered advice on navigating life in the UK, covering everything from local events to practical tips for adapting to a new environment.

As Olakunle finished scanning the last of her items, a brief pause settled over him. He reached for a piece of paper from a drawer behind the counter and quickly scribbled down his telephone number. "If you ever need assistance or just want to chat, feel free to reach out," he said, his tone warm and inviting. "I'm always here to lend an ear. Don't hesitate to contact me anytime."

Yetunde's heart fluttered with a blend of relief and uncertainty. She glanced at the piece of paper he offered, her mind swirling with conflicting thoughts. While the gesture was undoubtedly kind and practical, she recognised the need to consider her personal boundaries. After a moment's hesitation, she accepted the paper, her fingers lightly grazing his as she took it, sending a slight shiver of awareness through her.

"Thank you, Olakunle," she said cautiously, her voice carrying a hint of uncertainty. "I'm grateful for your kindness."

As Olakunle waited for Yetunde to bag her groceries before attending to the next customer, but she could not shake the sensation of his intense stare. He seemed focused on her chest, his eyes lingering there as she hurriedly stuffed the items into the bag. The weight of his gaze made her increasingly uncomfortable, and she found herself rushing through the task, eager to finish and escape the unsettling feeling of his attention. It was as though she could feel his eyes on her, pressing into her skin, making every movement feel overly exposed.

Yetunde quickly made her way back to the care home as soon as she tucked the last item into the bag, each step filled with a mix of anticipation and unease. The conversation they'd shared had been unexpectedly pleasant—perhaps too pleasant. There was a subtle charm in Olakunle's words, a warmth that enveloped her like a cosy blanket, making her feel seen in a way she hadn't experienced in a long time. However, as she walked, a nagging tension settled in her chest, leaving her feeling uneasy. The intensity of his attention, combined with her growing sense of vulnerability, was unsettling.

Her mind began to churn with questions. Was it the stress of her demanding shifts, or was there something more at play? The stirring emotions she had tried to ignore now lingered, intertwining with the uncertainty in her heart. A part of her longed for the validation and connection that Olakunle had offered, but she also knew that crossing that line would jeopardise everything she held dear—her family, her marriage, and the life she was trying to build in this new country with Afolabi. Yetunde felt torn, caught between the allure of something unexpected and the reality of her commitments.

The piece of paper in her hand felt like a tangible symbol of the new connections she was forging; yet, it also served as a reminder of the delicate balance she needed to maintain between being friendly and staying true to her principles. For a moment, she considered squeezing it and tossing it into the bin, rejecting the possibility it represented. But something stopped her. As she returned to her duties, she promised herself this would be the last time she entertained any thoughts of Olakunle beyond a simple exchange. Her focus had to remain on Afolabi and their journey together.

After her encounter with Olakunle at the till the previous night, Yetunde could not shake the memory of his warm smile and easygoing friendliness. There was something about his approach that felt distinct. Their conversation had been innocent enough- a brief exchange about their shared Nigerian heritage and how rare it was to meet someone from the same tribe. Yet, as she went about her duties that night, his words lingered in her mind longer than they should have, creating an unsettling feeling within her.

The following night, during her break from work, Yetunde decided to send Olakunle a message. It wasn't anything serious, just a brief thank-you for their conversation and an attempt to establish some boundaries. After all, she was happily married, and Afolabi had always treated her with kindness. Taking a deep breath, she typed out the text.

"Hi Olakunle, I wanted to thank you for your kind words yesterday. It was nice to talk to someone from home. By the way, I'm happily married, and I thought it best to mention that so we're both clear on our boundaries. Have a great night!"

Olakunle's reply arrived only a few minutes later, and his smooth, confident tone sent a wave of unease through Yetunde.

"Hey, Yetunde! I totally understand, and I promise I'm not that kind of guy. I really enjoy connecting with people who share the same background, and I completely respect boundaries. Just two Nigerians catching up in a foreign land, nothing to worry about!"

Yetunde felt a wave of relief as she read his reply. Maybe she had overreacted. She shook her head, almost laughing at herself. "See?" she thought, a hint of amusement in her mind. "There's nothing to worry about. It's just a casual acquaintance." The tension that had tightened her chest began to ease as she reassured herself, allowing a small smile to play on her lips.

The week passed without any interaction between them, though Yetunde spotted Olakunle in ASDA just four days after their first encounter. As she entered the supermarket to pick up groceries for one of the residents, she noticed him at one of the tills. A mix of emotions swirled within her, but she chose to keep her distance, simply waving at him from afar. She intentionally went for self-checkout to avoid having him attend to her, doing everything she could to maintain the boundaries she had established while still acknowledging their shared connection.

However, as the days passed, Olakunle, with his smooth charm and easy confidence, seemed to know exactly when to reach out. He sent her occasional texts that chipped away at her resolve, each message casual on the surface, as if they were nothing more than friends. Yetunde could not shake the sense of flirtation that crept into his words, an undertone that made her heart race despite her attempts to remain indifferent. Although she never responded to any of those texts, however, the more Olakunle reached out, the harder it became for her to resist the allure of his charm.

Yetunde found herself going through Olakunle's text messages during break times and thinking about him more than she cared to admit. Life had settled into a monotonous cycle of long shifts, exhaustion, and a growing emotional distance between her and Afolabi. Their time together had diminished, leaving them with little more than brief exchanges about caring for the twins or work responsibilities during their one or two nights off together each week. The loneliness gnawed at her; a persistent ache that felt unfamiliar. While she had always prided herself on her independence, this was different; it left her feeling isolated in a way she could neither identify nor understand.

Olakunle's persistence was subtle yet persuasive. He never pushed too hard, understanding that patience was his greatest weapon. His words reminded her of the attention she craved, the attention that had been lacking at home with Afolabi, as their lives revolved around work, bills, and the daily grind. Olakunle offered her a glimpse of something different—something thrilling in its simplicity. And that was what scared her most.

Three weeks after her first encounter with Olakunle, at around 9:30 PM, Yetunde had just finished another one-on-one session with a resident. The calm of the night shift surrounded her, offering a moment of peace as she leaned against the counter, allowing herself to embrace the silence and feeling the weight of the night begin to lift. Just as she was about to take a breath and gather her thoughts, her phone vibrated, jolting her back to the present and drawing her attention.

She picked up the phone from her trouser pocket, expecting a routine message from a colleague or perhaps a quick reminder from Afolabi. Instead, her heart raced at the sight of Olakunle's number glowing on the screen, stirring a mix of excitement and uncertainty within her. Curious, she unlocked her phone to read his words, wondering what had prompted him to reach out to her at that time of the night. This time, it was not just a casual greeting or a brief check-in. Instead, it was a subtle invitation.

"Hey Yetunde, how have you been? I know things have been hectic, but I thought of you today. Are you working tonight? If you're on break, it would be lovely to catch up and relax for a bit. Perhaps you could stop by? No pressure, of course. Just two friends hanging out."

The message lingered on her screen, her thumb hovering over the reply button. The invitation seemed harmless enough after a particularly difficult night at work, yet she understood its deeper implications. It was not just two friends talking; it signified the start of something more— something that could lead her down a path she had vowed never to tread.

Yetunde stared at the message for what felt like an eternity. She thought of Afolabi and the life they had built together. Despite the distance between them, she still loved him. However, the excitement she felt when thinking about Olakunle—the thrill of being seen in a different light—was hard to ignore. It was a feeling she hadn't experienced in a long time, and the allure was almost intoxicating.

She knew she should delete the message, block Olakunle, and walk away from this temptation once and for all. Yet, something stopped her. Maybe it was the longing for a moment of escape, or perhaps it was the fear of being trapped in a routine that had slowly chipped away at her happiness. Whatever it was, Yetunde found herself typing a reply before she could stop herself.

"Thanks, Olakunle. I've been busy." She suddenly stopped, and her heart skipped a beat as she stared at the message again. An odd mix of flattery and discomfort churned within her. She had not expected to hear from him again, and a flutter of hesitation crept in. "What did he want?" The question nagged at her as she hesitated, contemplating her response.

"Yes, I'm at work tonight", she typed slowly, considering her words. "But I don't think it's a good idea to meet. I usually spend my breaks resting rather than entertaining anything else."

She hit send, feeling a state of anticipation and a slight sense of unease.

Olakunle responded almost instantly, his words laced with playful insistence. "Come on, Yetunde! Just for a few minutes. It's not every day I get to see a friendly face at work. You deserve a break. It's simply a quick chat!" he urged playfully. "I promise, no stress. I know you must be tired, but a friendly face might lift your spirits."

She was still contemplating how to respond when his next message arrived.

"I know you're a responsible woman," he continued his tone a blend of playfulness and sincerity. "But just for five minutes? I promise I won't keep you long. Besides, I don't want you to think I'm a difficult guy to deal with. You're making me look bad here!"

Yetunde bit her lip, wrestling with her thoughts. She knew she should say no; there was no real reason to go to ASDA or meet him, let alone at that time of the night. But a part of her—perhaps the part that felt neglected in her own marriage—longed for the attention and connection. She shook her head, scolding herself for even considering it, feeling a mix of guilt and the desire within her.

She hesitated once more, caught in a web of conflicting emotions. She did not want to appear difficult or unfriendly, yet deep down, she knew this was not a good idea. Still, the tug of curiosity and the subtle flattery in his messages wore her down, drawing her in despite her better judgment. "Alright, just for a few minutes," she typed reluctantly, her heart racing at the prospect. "I'll stop by at 11:40 PM."

As she sent the message, Yetunde took a steadying breath, feeling a mix of excitement and uncertainty. She reminded herself it was just a quick, friendly chat, nothing more. But as 11:40 pm approached, she could not ignore the flutter in her chest—a feeling she had not expected from such a simple meeting.

When the time finally came, she slipped away for her break, her thoughts swirling in anticipation as she made her way to the 24-hour ASDA.

Yetunde arrived at ASDA, feeling a mix of guilt and nervousness. Her break was only an hour, and she had already wasted precious minutes deliberating whether to come or not. It was as if Olakunle had been waiting for her as he met her at the entrance, a broad smile lighting up his face as she approached. His casual confidence sent an unsettling ripple through her, a feeling she could not quite articulate.

"Hey, sis," he greeted her, his voice warm and welcoming as he walked toward her. "I'm really glad you could make it."

"Hi," Yetunde replied, her smile faint and hesitant, a flicker of uncertainty in her eyes. "I can't stay" long." "That's alright,"

Olakunle replied smoothly, motioning for her to come outside. "Let's head over there—it's quieter. Besides, it's getting chilly out here. You can sit in the car and relax while we chat."

Yetunde hesitated, her instincts urging her to leave. However, something about Olakunle's relaxed demeanour made it difficult to say no. He opened the car door for her and waited until she was settled inside before closing it. As she slipped into the car, the warm scent of his cologne enveloped her, drawing her in despite her reservations.

As they sat in the car, Olakunle leaned back, his gaze lingering on her in a way that made Yetunde feel both noticed and uncomfortably exposed. Initially, their conversation revolved around safe, mundane topics—work and the challenges of adapting to life in the UK—but gradually, the tone shifted. The words grew more personal, edging closer to a space Yetunde was uncertain she wanted to enter.

"You're a really strong woman, Yetunde," Olakunle said, his voice dropping to a softer, more intimate tone. "I can see it in you. It must be tough balancing everything as you do. Sometimes, I wonder how you manage it all."

"Any man would be lucky to have someone like you," he said, his words laced with admiration and something more lingering in the air between them.

"Yetunde's heart raced, a wave of tension settling between them. She shifted uncomfortably in her seat, feeling the pressure of the moment build.

"I should really get back to work soon," she said, her voice wavering as she tried to create distance between them.

Olakunle leaned in slightly, his voice taking on a more flirtatious edge. "Just a few more minutes," he persuaded softly. "You're too tense—relax a little. It's just you and me here." Yetunde opened her mouth to respond, but the words faltered as Olakunle's hand brushed against hers. She flinched slightly, her heart racing, but she did not pull away. He smiled gently, his hand now resting on hers, his eyes locking onto hers with an intensity that sent a shiver down her spine. "You know, you're even more beautiful up close," he murmured, his voice soft and sincere. He leaned in just a little closer, the warmth of his presence surrounding her, making the air between them feel palpable.

Yetunde's mind screamed at her to leave, but something invisible held her rooted to the spot. She did not want to encourage him, yet the attention was undeniably intoxicating—a heady elixir she hadn't realised she had been craving. Each lingering moment only deepened her internal conflict, drawing her closer to the warmth of his gaze, even as every part of her wished to pull away.

Olakunle's face moved in closer, and before she could fully process what was happening, he leaned in to kiss her. Instinctively, Yetunde pulled back, shaking her head with urgency. "No... I can't do this," she said, her voice trembling as she fought to regain her composure.

"Hey, it's just a kiss," Olakunle said smoothly, his voice low and persuasive, as he leaned in slightly closer. "No one's getting hurt. I just wanted to show you how I feel."

Yetunde's breath came in short, quick bursts as she whispered, "I'm married." The weight of her words hung heavily in the air. Her heart pounded in her chest as she grappled with the burden of the confession, the gravity of the situation pressing down on her.

"And I respect that," Olakunle replied, his voice steady and almost soothing. He did not pull back, his gaze soft yet intense. "But that doesn't mean we can't have a moment. Just you and me."

For a moment, Yetunde's mind became paralysed in a storm of conflicting thoughts, torn between desire and guilt. Then, before she could stop herself, she leaned in, and their lips met—a brief, electric connection. It was over almost as soon as it began, but the wave of regret that followed hit her like a flood, leaving her breathless and consumed with uncertainty.

She pulled back sharply, her eyes wide with shock and self-loathing. "No. How could I do this?" she muttered, her voice trembling as she fumbled with the car door handle. "I have to go." The words tumbled out, each one heavy with regret, as she fought to reclaim her thoughts.

"Yetunde, wait," Olakunle called out, his voice urgent yet tinged with frustration. Tension thickened the air, creating a silent pull between them, a mixture of confusion and longing. He tried to reach for her, his hand outstretched, desperate to close the gap she was creating. But she was already out of the car, her feet striking the pavement hard as she stormed away. Her mind raced with guilt, shame, and disgust at her actions. She felt as if she had betrayed Afolabi—and herself. The cold night air hit her like a slap to the face, but it couldn't wash away the overwhelming weight of betrayal that pressed heavily on her chest.

As she hurried back to work, tears welled up in her eyes, blurring her vision. How could she have let this happen? The questions spiralled in her mind, each one sharper than the last. How could she possibly face Afolabi now, knowing she had crossed a line she never intended to breach? Her chest tightened under the weight of it all. She forced herself to focus, summoning the strength to maintain her composure throughout the shift. But no matter how hard she tried, the guilt pressed down on her like an unrelenting weight, a constant reminder of the line she had crossed and the trust she had lost.

As Olakunle sat in his car after she stormed away, a smug smile curled at the corners of his lips. He understood women like Yetunde—strong on the outside yet undeniably vulnerable when given the right kind of attention. She was a challenge, and Olakunle thrived on challenges. The fact that she was married only heightened the thrill of the conquest, igniting a dangerous excitement within him. He relished the thought of breaking down her defences, using his words, actions, and shrewdness to unravel her, before savouring the sweet taste of victory that lay just within reach, only to dump her for another prey.

The kiss had been a victory—a triumph of charm over restraint. He had sensed Yetunde's initial reluctance and hesitation, yet he was confident that he could dismantle her defences with just the right amount of allure and charm.

"I still got the vibes," he told himself proudly, admiring his reflection in the car mirror. And he was right. That brief kiss had been proof enough that she was not as unattainable as she pretended to be; it provided a tantalising glimpse into the possibility of winning her over completely.

He would not rush it, though. Olakunle sensed that Yetunde was grappling with guilt, and he knew that pushing her too hard too soon would only drive her away. No, patience was key. He needed to give her space and let her come to him on her own terms. He had already planted the seed of temptation, and now he just had to wait for it to take root and flourish. He was not new to the game; he understood the delicate balance of allure and distance. The more he played it cool and allowed her to wrestle with her own feelings, the more irresistible he would become. All in due time.

Chapter 6

Rumours and Doubts

Yetunde sat at the edge of the bed, her heart pounding in the silence of the house around her. The kiss from Olakunle played over and over in her mind, like a film reel she could not stop. Each replay was a vivid reminder of the moment when everything shifted. It had not been planned, but for a fleeting instant, it felt as if she had stepped into another life—a life unburdened by the roles of wife and mother.

But just as quickly as the rush of excitement had come, it faded, replaced by a deep, gnawing guilt. How had she allowed herself to fall so far? Afolabi didn't deserve this betrayal—he had always been there for her, even when she pulled away. And yet, a part of her craved more. More freedom. More excitement. The very thing she had hoped to find in the UK now felt like a heavy burden, dragging her in ways she didn't want to go.

What was wrong with her?

Burying her face in her hands, she felt the weight of her secret pressing down on her chest, suffocating her. She could not tell him. Not now. Not ever. The shame was too much to bear, yet the silence was oppressive.

The day shift at the care home was bustling with activity, a stark contrast to the calmer atmosphere Yetunde sometimes experienced during her night shifts. While the stillness of the night offered a semblance of peace, it was no less demanding. Residents still required constant care, medications had to be administered, and routine tasks—checking vitals and ensuring comfort for those who struggled to sleep—kept her occupied. Although the pace may have slowed compared to the daytime rush, the responsibilities never ceased.

Afolabi gracefully moved through the lively corridors, where the animated conversations of residents blended with the vibrant energy of the surroundings, creating a captivating atmosphere. It had been a tiring week, and today, he was paired with Thomas, one of the few colleagues with whom he had developed a genuine bond since joining New Heritage Care Home. Whenever Thomas was on the day shift, they often took time during their breaks to share stories and aspirations, providing a welcome respite from the hectic pace of the day.

As Afolabi entered the staff break room, he noticed Thomas was already there, calmly enjoying his lunch of beans and fried plantain. The room was cosy, with a couple of couches, a table filled with magazines, and a plasma TV on the wall. Afolabi picked up his lunch from the fridge and sat opposite him.

"Looks like it's going to be a long day," Afolabi commented, pausing to sip his coffee. "Yeah," Thomas replied, his voice lacking its usual enthusiasm. He appeared preoccupied; his attention focused on the table. After a moment, he looked up at Afolabi, concern etched on his face

"Afolabi, there's something important I need to discuss with you."

Afolabi looked at Thomas, sensing the seriousness in his friend's tone. "What's the matter, Thomas? You look...worried."

Thomas hesitated, clearly uneasy with the subject he was about to bring up. It's about Yetunde."

"Which Yetunde?" Afolabi asked, a hint of confusion in his voice as he tried to grasp the seriousness of Thomas' words.

"Your wife, Yetunde," Thomas replied, his voice

laced with reluctance. "I feel uneasy bringing this up, but... I witnessed something a few nights ago."

Afolabi's heart raced, but he fought to maintain his composure. "What are you trying to say? What did you see?"

Thomas leaned in closer, his voice barely above a whisper, as if he feared being overheard despite the empty room. "It was late, around 11p.m or so. I was walking past the ASDA car park at the end of my shift when I saw Yetunde in a car with a guy."

Afolabi's forehead creased in confusion as he tried to understand Thomas' words. "In a car? Thomas, are you certain it was Yetunde?"

Thomas nodded; his face filled with concern. "She was the one, Afolabi. I am absolutely certain. Don't I know Yetunde, your wife again? What type of question is that? They had a deep connection, perhaps too deep. It seemed to be more than just a casual conversation."

Afolabi was hit by a sudden wave of unease, but he fought to dismiss it, unwilling to let the

unsettling thoughts take root in his mind. "What do you mean by too deep?" he asked, trying to maintain his composure.

"Thomas, that doesn't seem right," he said, his voice filled with disbelief. "I can take everything else from you, but not you saying Yetunde is cheating on me." Are you absolutely certain you're not mistaken?"

Thomas shook his head firmly, conviction etched across his face. "No, Afolabi, she was the one. I had a clear view from where I was standing when she stepped out of the car. They were... well, they were kissing. Right there in the car park lot."

Afolabi's breath caught in his throat, yet he managed to maintain his composure. "Smooching? Thomas, you should be more familiar with Yetunde. There's no way she would do something like that. Perhaps it was an individual who bore a striking resemblance to her. People frequently make errors when they cannot see clearly, especially at night."

Thomas let out a deep breath, reclining in his chair. "Afolabi, I want to assure you that what I'm about to say is true. I am confident in my observations. And I'm sorry to be the one to mention it, but... you really should have a conversation with her."

Afolabi sensed the influencing pressure, yet he resisted the encroaching uncertainty. He had complete faith in Yetunde and was determined not to let a single night of doubt shatter that trust. "Thomas," he stated confidently, "I appreciate your concern, but I know my wife well. I can trust Yetunde; she will never betray me. Whatever you witnessed, it was not what you

think."

Thomas stared at him silently, seemingly holding back his thoughts. "Alright, Afolabi," he finally said, his voice filled with acceptance. "I just felt it was important to let you know about it."

You're a kind-hearted individual, and I would hate to see any harm come your way." Afolabi mustered a smile, attempting to brighten the atmosphere.

"I understand, Thomas. Rest assured, there is no cause for concern. Let's just focus on getting through this." shift."

Thomas nodded; his eyes still filled with concern. "Alright." But if you ever need someone to talk to, I'm here for you."

"Thanks," Afolabi replied, returning to his lunch, even though he had lost his appetite. Thomas' words echoed in his mind as they resumed their responsibilities, casting a shadow he could not quite shake. The lingering doubt gnawed at him, no matter how hard he tried to push it away.

But as they resumed their work, Afolabi attempted to dispel the discomfort that had taken hold of him. He reassured himself that it was merely a miscommunication, believing that Yetunde could never descend so low as to be with a man in a car park. However, no matter how hard he tried, a persistent voice in the depths of his thoughts continued to replay Thomas' words.

At the end of his long day shift, Afolabi stepped outside into the refreshing evening breeze, a fleeting relief amidst the lingering sense of unease. He glanced over at the car park where Thomas had claimed to have seen Yetunde, his eyes drawn to the very spot Thomas had indicated. The silence of the evening seemed to amplify his racing thoughts; each breath felt heavy with doubt. He took a deep breath, attempting to reaffirm his strong faith in his wife. Yetunde had been his steadfast support through all the highs and lows, and he was resolute in his determination to keep any uncertainty at bay.

However, as he made his way home, the vivid image of Yetunde in that vehicle, as recounted by Thomas, lingered in his mind like a haunting shadow. He tried to convince himself it was nothing more than a case of mistaken identity, a fleeting moment exaggerated beyond its worth. Yet, as he approached their modest flat and saw the warm glow of the lights within, the comfort he had longed for seemed to vanish. He hesitated at the door for a moment, grappling with the turmoil raging inside him. Taking a deep breath, he retrieved the key from his pocket and stepped inside, determined to safeguard the life he was resolute in defending, no matter the obstacles ahead.

The moment he entered, his twin daughters jumped on him and wouldn't let go. This was their usual way of welcoming him. "Ekabo!" they chirped sweetly like two songbirds. Despite his tiredness, he squatted down, lifting both of them into his arms, spinning around with them a couple of times before gently setting them down. Afterwards, he sank into the couch, closing his eyes to rest.

"Daddy, tell us one of those moonlight stories you used to tell us," One of the twins said, tapping his left arm gently.

"Yes, Daddy, we want to hear another one now," the other twin said.

"I will, but not right now. Daddy needs to rest."

"You promise?" asked Dami, who often spoke with the seriousness of an adult.

"I promise. I'll tell you about the giant white wicked bird."

At the mention of the story, the girls squealed with excitement and ran off to play.

Chapter 7

Allure and Regret

After that initial meeting with Olakunle, Yetunde found herself caught in a whirlwind of conflicting emotions. Overwhelmed by a strong sense of regret, she began to withdraw and isolate herself at home. In Afolabi's presence, she became increasingly subdued, her once vibrant energy dampened by the weight of her remorse. Hesitating to make eye contact, she feared he might sense her vulnerability and the guilt she felt.

Every time it surfaced, she recoiled, her stomach twisting in knots of regret. What made it worse was the nagging awareness that she had seen the red flags from the very beginning. She had sensed that Olakunle wasn't simply being friendly; there was an undercurrent behind his smooth words and persistent charm. Yet, she had chosen to ignore those instincts, allowing herself to fall into his trap. In those moments of reflection, she felt foolish and weak, grappling with the shame of her choices. Afolabi observed a shift in her demeanour but attributed it to the demanding nature of their care jobs and the long hours they both put in. He enquired about her well-being, but Yetunde nodded, attempting to smile despite the lack of sincerity in her eyes. "I'm just exhausted," she mentioned, and Afolabi, not wanting to press further, decided to drop the subject.

Late one night, unable to sleep, Yetunde sat up in bed, her gaze drifting to Afolabi, who lay beside her, breathing softly in his sleep. She reached for her phone, her eyes locking onto Olakunle's number. A wave of nausea swept over her at the sight. Her thumb hovered over the delete button, her heart racing as guilt and anger twisted inside her.

For a long moment, she hesitated, torn between desire and shame. Finally, with a shaky breath, she pressed "delete." It felt like a small action, but it was a step—a quiet act of reclaiming her integrity, a flicker of resolve amid the chaos of her emotions. However, that wasn't enough to silence the guilt that still gnawed at her, a persistent reminder of the line she had crossed.

As the days passed, Yetunde found herself drifting further away from Afolabi. The weight of her guilt pressed down on her more heavily with each passing day, creating an invisible chasm between them. She blamed herself, fully aware that this was not Afolabi's fault. He had done nothing wrong. Yet, each time he looked at her with those trusting eyes, she felt as if she were suffocating beneath the crushing weight of the betrayal she carried within. The guilt twisted like a knife in her gut, amplifying her shame and deepening the chasm between them.

Yetunde recalled that night in the car with Olakunle, a painful reminder of her moment of weakness and loneliness. She had let her guard down, and he had exploited that vulnerability. Yet, she could not deny that a part of her had been flattered by his attention—the way he had made her feel seen and valued, something she hadn't experienced in a long time. She cursed herself for even entertaining those thoughts, for allowing that fleeting moment of connection to linger in her mind like a shadow, taunting her with the warmth she craved but had betrayed.

She placed her head back on her pillow and fell asleep, tears of regret streaming down the pillowcase. The weight of her actions pressed heavily on her chest; each tear a silent reminder of her inaction. In the quiet darkness, her heart ached with the knowledge that sleep might offer some escape but not the peace she longed for.

The following morning, Yetunde was still consumed by a heavy sense of guilt. The memory of Olakunle's kiss remained vivid in her mind, an exhilarating sensation she could not shake off. It lingered, particularly in moments of solitude when her thoughts drifted. A powerful urge to confess and unburden herself rose within her, but the fear of jeopardising her marriage to Afolabi and causing him pain kept her silent. She made a quiet vow to herself that it would never happen again, deciding to leave Olakunle behind and focus on her family and the life she had built with Afolabi.

Despite her best efforts to suppress it, the allure of Olakunle's kiss lingered. It grew stronger, like an invisible pull, eroding her resolve. She could not escape the feeling that Olakunle had somehow enchanted her with that kiss, leaving a lasting trace in her mind. The emotional weight of her internal conflict made her feel unclean, torn between the life she believed she should lead and the temptation to yield to the potent memories of that night. Yet, no matter how hard she tried, she could not rid herself of the thoughts of him.

This inner turmoil began to take a toll on her daily life, causing Yetunde to withdraw even further. She found herself distancing from Afolabi, resisting his touch, and avoiding intimacy. When he reached out to her in bed, she feigned sleep, unable to connect with him. Their relationship, already strained by the demands of their busy lives, started to fray further. Afolabi tried to reach out, attempting to understand her emotional distance, but the gap between them only widened. Meanwhile, the emotional pull of Olakunle seemed to fill the space that Afolabi's attempts at connection had once occupied.

In the days that followed, he sent her the occasional text—nothing overly flirtatious, just casual greetings and friendly check-ins to see how she was doing. He was careful not to come across as too eager; that would only push her away. His goal was to remain present in her thoughts, subtly reminding her that he was still there, a possibility waiting in the wings if she ever wanted more. Each time her phone buzzed with a message from him, she deleted it immediately without a second thought, her hand trembling slightly as she did so. His messages now served as a painful reminder of her shame—a stark reminder that she had betrayed Afolabi in a way she had never imagined possible. She hesitated to block his number as if doing so would erase the reality of what had happened. Instead, ignoring him felt like her only means of reclaiming control, a way to protect herself from the guilt that threatened to engulf her.

Whenever she visited ASDA to buy groceries for the residents, Yetunde made a conscious effort to avoid the tills, opting for self-checkout to steer clear of Olakunle. She would linger at the back, pretending to browse the shelves until she was sure he wasn't around. However, now and then, their paths would unavoidably cross. Each time, he greeted her with that same disarming smile, but she kept her responses short and almost dismissive, her heart racing as she fought to maintain her composure. "Hey, Yetunde. How have you been?" His voice carried that same casual charm, effortlessly inviting, yet she refused to meet his gaze.

"Fine," she muttered, her eyes intentionally avoiding him, fixated on the ground or the shelves behind him, anywhere but on his face.

Her responses were terse, her tone icy, yet Olakunle remained undeterred. If anything, her resistance only fueled his desire. He regarded her as a puzzle—one he was certain he could solve given time.

Olakunle could tell that Yetunde was deliberately avoiding him. He watched her closely, sensing the guilt that seemed to hang in the air around her as if she were battling with her own conscience. However, he also recognised that the attention he had given her had awakened something more—an unspoken longing for validation, excitement, and a break from the monotony of her everyday life.

Meanwhile, Olakunle patiently bided his time. He knew Yetunde was trying to distance herself, but he also understood that the more she resisted, the more she would think about him. Each time their paths crossed, he saw the conflict in her eyes—torn between her loyalty to Afolabi and the undeniable pull between them. "She'll surely come back to me," he muttered to himself one evening, his eyes gleaming with a mixture of arrogance and confidence.

He planned to send her another text soon, but he knew he had to tread carefully. He needed to remind her that he was still present, patiently waiting for her to reconsider. His aim was to stoke the flames of her curiosity and frustration, keeping her intrigued. This was not just about sharing another kiss; it was about possessing her completely, conquering her heart and mind in a way that would leave no room for doubt.

The tension between Yetunde and Afolabi at home thickened, settling over them like a heavy fog. She meticulously avoided his questions about her night shifts, providing only vague, one-word responses that felt like walls closing in around them. Afolabi couldn't shake the nagging feeling that something was terribly wrong. Yet, each time he tried to probe deeper, Yetunde deflected with a strained smile, leaving him feeling more isolated and uneasy than ever

"I'm just tired, Afolabi. It's nothing," she would say, though her eyes told a different story, flickering with unspoken fears and hidden guilt. Sensing her reluctance to discuss it further, Afolabi chose to drop the subject, swallowing his concerns and allowing the silence to linger like a heavy weight between them.

Evening, the weight of guilt overwhelmed Yetunde. She found herself pacing back and forth in the small living room, her mind restless. Afolabi was busy with his work from home while the girls peacefully slumbered in their room. Once again, she contemplated sharing her entire story with him, releasing the burden of the hidden truth that was gradually consuming her. However, she was acutely aware of the implications. The strong bond they had developed, the deep affection they had cultivated over time, and the trust he had in her would all be irrevocably shattered, and for what purpose? Feeling vulnerable?

Instead, she chose to confide in Adenike, her trusted friend and a mental health nurse at King George Hospital in Goodmayes, Ilford. Adenike had been her closest friend since they were in nursing school back in Nigeria. She was one of the few individuals Yetunde trusted completely, and she knew she needed someone to lean on—someone who could help her navigate the tangled web of emotions she found herself caught in.

The following day, they met at a Turkish restaurant on Whalebone Lane North in Dagenham, not far from Adenike's house. It was a gloomy Saturday afternoon, the kind of day that heightened Yetunde's sense of solitude in this unfamiliar place. The restaurant's warm, inviting atmosphere offered a comforting refuge from the dreary weather outside. However, a feeling of unease still lingered within Yetunde, unsettling her as she prepared to share her burden.

Adenike arrived a few minutes later, radiating her usual energy and enthusiasm. She embraced

Yetunde warmly, her cheerful expression contrasting with Yetunde's gloomy demeanour. They ordered Turkish pizza with diced lamb and peppers and settled into a quiet corner of the restaurant. Yetunde took a sip from her drink and let out a deep breath, summoning the courage to open up to her trusted friend about her burdens.

"Adenike, there's something I need to confess... something that I deeply regret," Yetunde began, her voice barely above a whisper. She gazed at her plate of food before her, avoiding eye contact with her friend.

Adenike's curiosity was piqued as she leaned in, raising an eyebrow. "What's happening, Yetunde? Feel free to share anything with me."

With a sigh, Yetunde reflected on the events of the past few weeks—the encounter with Olakunle, the exchanged messages, the shared coffee, and, ultimately, the unexpected kiss in the car park.

"Adenike, back in Nigeria, I never starved. It felt like telepathic communication between us; whenever I wanted it or even felt like it, he was always ready to satisfy me. He was so romantic, so loving. Ever since our relocation here, the story has changed completely.

Sometimes, I wonder if he has lost his manhood, except on very rare occasions when he is truly happy." As she spoke, Yetunde pulled her black leather handbag closer, gripping it tightly as if afraid of losing something. Then, she stifled a yawn, momentarily loosening her hold to cover her mouth before continuing.

"Many times, I've tried to seduce him, hinting at my need for it, but he never stirred nor noticed a woman beside him, leaving me to burn endlessly. The most he sometimes does is reach out and squeeze my hand tenderly, which only intensifies my longing, yet without satisfaction. All he talks about, day and night, in front of his computer, is software, software, programming, programming. 'I've made a breakthrough in this!' 'Oh, I've made a breakthrough in that!' It's like he's obsessed with it; he seems more excited about his programming than about me. He even invites me to look at his screen, his face lighting up with excitement as if he'd just experienced an orgasm. I wish he'd redirect that thrill into our sexual and romantic life instead of giving it all to his work."

At that moment, Adenike almost burst out laughing. She pressed her lips together tightly, trying to hold it in so that Yetunde wouldn't notice. "When he finally got the job, we were overjoyed—

he was ecstatic. As soon as he told me, I rushed out of the kitchen and threw my arms around him. In that moment, when he held me close, I was overwhelmed with desire and expectation. But to my great disappointment, he pulled away and left me hanging, stepping off to make some phone calls. He completely avoided any discussion about what had just happened, leaving me in a state of emotional confusion. I spent the next few days in a daze, struggling to focus on anything. Thankfully, my professional training helped me keep it together at work, though I was emotionally distracted and restless.

The night before I met with Olakunle, I resolved to set aside my pride and directly ask for what I needed, hoping to confront the situation. However, things didn't go as planned. Just as I was walking into the house, he was leaving. He approached me, looked into my eyes with affection, and said, "Hey, baby, you look tired. Please, rest well and take care." Then he squeezed my hand tenderly, just as he always does, and walked away. I nearly burst into tears.

Look, Adenike, when he approached me, I thought at the very least he would kiss me or show some affection—but no. My mind was on fire. Actually, not just my mind—everything felt like it was burning. That evening, I wasn't myself; I was utterly uncoordinated. Just as I was about to lose control, this man appeared at the perfect moment. I don't know what it was, but I felt an unexpected ease around him, a comfort I hadn't experienced before. Was it because he shared certain traits with Afolabi, my husband? Whatever it was, it led me down a messy path I never knew how to navigate imagined."

As she spoke, she sensed a burden being lifted from her shoulders, yet the lingering shame persisted, unwilling to let go.

After finishing her story, a heavy silence filled the air. Yetunde looked up, bracing herself for disappointment in Adenike's eyes. Instead, she saw understanding, perhaps even a hint of amusement.

"Yetunde, you're overthinking it," Adenike said, her tone casual yet reassuring. "Do you have any idea how many women are in similar situations? There's nothing wrong with seeking a little excitement, especially given all the challenges we face here in Europe." Yetunde was taken aback by her friend's unexpected response.

However, ... I'm Yetunde, and I'm happily married. I disagree with this. I feel I have betrayed Afolabi."

Adenike nonchalantly shrugged. "Listen, Yetunde, it's time to stop being so hard on yourself. We are presently in the UK, not our home country of Nigeria. There is a distinct contrast in this place. It's widely recognised how challenging it can be - constantly working, sending money back home, with little opportunity to spend quality time with our husbands and lacking affection.

You're simply filling a gap."

Yetunde stared at her friend in astonishment, struggling to grasp her words. "Filling a gap?"

"Yes, indeed, there's a gap," Adenike reiterated, leaning back in her chair with a hint of playful confidence. "Let me burst your bubble—some women even pay guys to fill those gaps." Adenike continued, reclining in her chair. "Consider this: how often do you and Afolabi actually spend time together?

You are on the night shift, and he works during the day. Given the various challenges in your life, your family's financial obligations, and the responsibilities of running a household, it's understandable that you may feel disconnected. It's all about work, work, work, with no time for personal connections. That's likely to compel anyone to find a way to cool down their mind before they run mad!"

Yetunde was embittered, as the words struck a personal chord. She reflected on the transformation their lives had undergone since relocating to the UK. The primary focus was consistently on work, ensuring financial stability, and meeting the expectations of family members in Nigeria. The chemistry that had once formed the foundation of her marriage had gradually diminished under the weight of these responsibilities.

Afolabi was a decent individual, but the limited time spent together, the lack of affection, and the unspoken strain of their new life had led to a sense of emptiness. "But this shouldn't be an excuse for her to misbehave," she told herself.

Adenike continued, her voice growing more solemn. "And it's crucial to remember that we're living in a country with its own set of legal protections. The culture here is distinctly different. Women have greater autonomy and wield more influence. If anything were to happen, the law is on your side. So, why should you feel guilty for prioritising your own well-being?"

Yetunde's mind was filled with a whirlwind of thoughts as she processed Adenike's words. The concept of "filling a gap" resonated with her in a way she had not anticipated. Indeed, ever since she arrived in the UK, her life had been consumed by an unending cycle of work and responsibility, leaving little room for the emotional connection she longed for. The obligations from her homeland, the expectations to provide for her family, and the clash between her cultural heritage and the challenges of living in the UK had all overwhelmed her.

Adenike's perspective, although surprising, provided a strangely reassuring sense of solace. It felt as though she was being granted approval to pursue what she had already accomplished, to persist in a course of action that had seemed misguided only moments earlier. The validation lifted a weight from her shoulders, allowing her to contemplate her own needs without the heavy burden of guilt.

However, deep inside, Yetunde was aware that her actions went beyond simply "filling a gap." It was a complete betrayal of the promises she had made to Afolabi, the Altar vow, and the deep love they had once shared. However, when confronted by the weight of Adenike's words, she began to doubt her promises. "Was their marriage already under strain due to the pressures of their new life? Didn't she deserve a bit of happiness, a break from the never-ending stress?"

As they finished their meal, Yetunde experienced

a complex blend of emotions—guilt, combined with a sense of justification and a risky feeling of validation. Adenike had sown a seed of uncertainty in her mind, one that would prove difficult to remove. The more she pondered it, the more the lines between right and wrong blurred, leaving her in a precarious position as she wrestled with her conscience.

As they said their goodbyes, Yetunde felt a fleeting sense of relief while waiting for Bus 103 towards Romford at the bus stop opposite Coventry University, London Campus in Dagenham. Yet, beneath that surface relief, her mind remained tangled in uncertainty and confusion. The guilt still lingered, stubborn and uninvited, even though Adenike's reassurances had softened its grip.

She had promised herself to prioritise her family and work on mending the fractures in her relationship, but the weight of her emotions remained as potent as before.

Yetunde found herself at a critical juncture, torn between the person she had been for so long and the one she was gradually becoming. As she stepped into the flat, welcomed by the joyful sounds of her daughters playing, she pushed aside any thoughts of Olakunle. However, later, as she got ready to go to work and bid Afolabi goodnight, the weight of her actions hung heavily upon her, casting a dark cloud that lingered over her every step. The choices she had made were irreversible, and that truth remained a constant, quiet reminder.

Chapter 8

Trials and Tribulations

The weeks following Yetunde's meeting with Adenike were incredibly challenging for Afolabi. Each day, the rumours distressed him, a relentless whisper that refused to fade. He found himself watching Yetunde more closely, searching for any sign—anything—that could either confirm or dismiss the growing uncertainties clouding his mind. The reassurances she had once offered, which had provided him with some comfort, now felt hollow and insufficient against the storm of doubt inside him. His love for her remained deep and resolute; however, alongside it, an unsettling sense of uncertainty had taken root, casting a shadow over their relationship that he could not shake off.

One evening, after yet another sleepless night, Afolabi came to a resolution. He desperately needed assistance and sought spiritual guidance to navigate the challenging path ahead. Feeling a weight on his shoulders, he scheduled a confidential meeting with Pastor Adewale, the man who had provided unwavering support to his family since they immigrated to the UK. If anyone could provide clarity, it would be him.

As Afolabi sat in the church's cosy, dimly lit office, he was still depressed despite his efforts to shake it off. The sweet fragrance of flowers from a nearby garden wafted in through the windows, and the walls were adorned with scripture passages, each offering a sense of hope and quietude. However, Afolabi's heart was far from at peace. He tightly gripped his hands, his thoughts racing as he struggled to find the perfect words to express the inner turmoil he was experiencing.

"Pastor, I—" His voice trembled, and he took a deep breath, trying to regain his composure. "I've been facing some challenges, Pastor. There are troubling rumours circulating about Yetunde... regarding her alleged extramarital affairs." He paused as a torrent of emotions surged within him, threatening to overwhelm his resolve. "I don't want to believe it, but... I can't seem to shake off the uncertainty."

Pastor Adewale regarded him with a calm and empathetic expression, his eyes reflecting a deep understanding of the anguish Afolabi was experiencing. He paused, allowing Afolabi's words to resonate in the silence that enveloped them.

"Afolabi," the pastor began, his voice filled with compassion and conviction, "marriage is a sacred union that flourishes through trust and faith. However, this bond can be tested by the challenges of the world, the doubts that creep in, and the everyday pressures we face. It's entirely normal to feel fear when those doubts arise, but it is crucial to ensure that fear does not overshadow the deep love you carry for your wife."

Afolabi nodded, his eyes downcast, feeling a mix of solace and embarrassment from the pastor's words. "I just... I deeply care for her, Pastor. I have strong feelings for her, and the idea of her being in a relationship with someone else deeply upsets me. I feel lost and unsure about my next steps."

"It is well, Brother Afolabi. If you don't mind, I'd like to ask a few questions that will help guide us toward some solutions. Your cooperation will be essential for us to achieve that."

"That is why I'm here, Pastor," Afolabi said

"How did you get married?"

"The normal way, Pastor." Afolabi promptly replied.

"We need to clarify a few things here," Pastor Adewale said, his voice steady yet gentle. "Let's start from the beginning. How did your relationship with Yetunde develop?" He gazed into Afolabi's eyes with the warmth of a caring father, seeking to understand the foundation of their bond.

Afolabi blinked his eyes twice, gathering his thoughts before responding. "If I understood your question correctly, Pastor, we got married as believers. We didn't cohabit as the unbelievers do. In fact, to the best of my knowledge, I am the first man in her life, and she is the only woman I've ever known and still know today."

The pastor moved closer, his features reflecting sincerity. "Afolabi, love encompasses more than just moments of joy and happiness. It's also about facing obstacles together and making the difficult choice to have faith. Adversaries will try to create division, seeking to instill doubt in your convictions. But it is important to maintain your faith."

"Have you had an open and honest conversation with Yetunde about this rumour?" Pastor Adewale asked, his gaze steady and encouraging. "Have you truly conveyed the depth of your fears to her?"

Afolabi shook his head, a deep sense of shame settling over him. "No, Pastor. I've been reluctant to mention it. I have no intention of making accusations or distancing myself from her. I am

determined to safeguard our family and preserve our current situation."

Pastor Adewale extended his hand, offering a comforting touch to Afolabi's shoulder. "Then go ahead and talk to her, Afolabi. Approach the situation with warmth and confidence, free from negative emotions or doubts. Marriage is like tending a garden, where constant care and attention are essential for its growth. Occasionally, we must address the doubts that may hinder its vitality, much like removing weeds that can suffocate it potential.

Most importantly, always remember to seek guidance from God. Hope for clarity, serenity in your heart, and resilience to confront any challenges that may arise."

Afolabi looked up, locking eyes with the pastor, sensing a glimmer of optimism amidst his inner turmoil.

"Thank you, Pastor. I really don't want to lose her. I really don't want to lose what we've built over the years."

"You won't," Pastor Adewale said with a reassuring smile. "There is a divine purpose behind your connection. Have faith in that, and have faith in one another. Love demonstrates patience and kindness. Rely on those truths; you will find the resilience to overcome any challenge. And there's something else I'd like you to note at this," point."

"What could that be, Pastor?" He asked excitedly.

"Let's turn to the Scriptures," the pastor said gently. "Bring out your Bible. If you don't have one with you, feel free to use your Bible App instead.

At this point, Afolabi felt utterly ashamed of himself. He couldn't remember the last time he had opened his Bible, let alone carried it around as he once did. The worst part was that even the Bible App, which had been a familiar icon on his phone, had vanished from his screen. It was as if he had drifted so far from his faith that even the slightest reminder was no longer within reach.

"Turn your Bible to Judges Chapter fourteen. Are you there?" Pastor Adewale asked, glancing up.

"Not yet." Afolabi admitted, feeling the heat rise to his cheeks.

"It's alright, use this one." He handed him a red-covered Bible from among an array of Bibles on his table and patiently waited for him to get to the place he quoted. This he did to save him further embarrassment when he saw how flustered he looked but pretended not to notice.

"I'm there now, Pastor," Afolabi said, his voice steadying.

"Good, you can read from verse one, but our main focus is on five and six."

Afolabi read through the passage and found it as intriguing as it had always been to him from his childhood and nothing special.

"Brother Afolabi, I want you to see the similarity of this passage to your case," he said, without raising his ebony face. He went on to explain how Samson, contrary to his parents' wishes, chose to marry a woman from Timnath, one of the daughters of the Philistines. Why? They believed he was acting wrongly, not realising he had God's approval. However, they eventually yielded to his pressure and accompanied him.

"Now comes the main issue, Brother Afolabi. When Samson was on the brink of his marriage, at the threshold of his ministry, just about to fulfil a purpose, the roar of a young lion emerged. Not an old, weak one, but a young, strong one!" He lifted his face and looked straight into Afolabi's eyes, continuing to expound on the passage. "At that moment, Samson seemed powerless and defenceless. And indeed, he was, for the Bible clearly states he had nothing in his hand. In this situation, he had no choice but to throw in the towel. How could he escape the paws or fangs of such a formidable enemy? But that was not the end of the story. Do you know what, Brother Afolabi?

"I'm listening, sir," he replied almost in a whisper, overwhelmed by Pastor Adewale's approach to the passage.

"That lion wasn't necessarily after Samson's flesh but his purpose. However, the good news is that a man of purpose cannot be swallowed! So, Samson turned to God, whose hand came upon him at that instant, and what should have scared him made him bold, what should have sunk him made him stand, and what should have weakened him made him strong. What was the result? He killed what would have killed him and eventually fed on what would have devoured him. You need God now more than ever to overcome this situation. Look at it this way: the IT job you've been seeking has just been offered, and now there's this situation. Stand firmly on the word of God and be strong in your prayers, and you'll sing of victory song."

"Thank you so much, Pastor; I can't really thank you enough. I should be leaving now," Afolabi said, feeling more relaxed.

"Before you go, let's have a word of prayer," Pastor Adewale said, continuing. "Thank you, dear Lord, for your ever-abiding presence with us. We call on your name to help us through this situation and grant us victory in Jesus' name." Amen."

As Afolabi left the church that evening, the burden on his shoulders seemed to have eased slightly. The pastor's words resonated in his thoughts, serving as a constant reminder of the deep affection he and Yetunde shared. Their love had faced numerous challenges in the past, yet it had always remained steadfast. He was resolute in his commitment to preserve that love and to defend his family fiercely with strong determination.

Returning home, Afolabi felt a fresh determination. He recognised the challenges ahead, but he was ready to confront them alongside Yetunde. The doubts might still linger, but with his unwavering faith as his compass, Afolabi was prepared to face any obstacles in his path, convinced that love would ultimately triumph.

Chapter 9

Confrontation and Conflict

The morning light filtered gently into the living room, casting long shadows across the floor. Afolabi sat on the edge of the couch, his hands tightly clasped together, knuckles white from the strain. He anxiously awaited Yetunde's return from her night shift, his heart weighed down with worry. Lost in thought, he was still trying to find the right words for their conversation when the front door creaked open, the sound soft but unmistakable in the stillness room.

Yetunde closed the door behind her, slipping off her shoes with a weary sigh, her eyes barely lifting to meet Afolabi's gaze. She moved toward the kitchen, her steps slow and heavy, her mind still clouded from the long night shift. However, Afolabi could not shake the growing urgency that had been troubling him all night. He sensed something was wrong—

an unspoken tension that had settled between them, tightening with each passing day, and now, it felt almost unbearable.

When she stepped out of the kitchen and into the living room, her weary expression revealed the toll that a sleepless night had taken on her. She appeared almost oblivious to his rigid posture, lost in the haze of exhaustion.

"Yetunde, we need to talk," Afolabi said softly, his voice revealing the turmoil of emotions brewing within him.

Yetunde paused, gently placing her bag on the nearest chair. Her eyes, both tired and cautious, met his gaze. "Afolabi, what's wrong?"

He gestured for her to sit beside him. As he observed her, he noticed the clear signs of concern etched on her face. He felt a profound sadness witnessing her in such a state, yet he could not overlook the seriousness of the situation and needed to address the underlying issues between them.

"I've noticed a change," he began, his tone cautious, almost delicate. "You seem to have been distant lately, appearing distracted and preoccupied," he stated, his voice laced with pain and confusion. "I feel like I'm losing you, Yetunde. I don't know what's happening between us, but I can sense it. I just can't...understand."

And then there are the rumours..." His voice faded away as if he didn't want to give too much weight to the words he was saying.

Yetunde looked puzzled. His words hit her with a force that made her throat tighten. "Rumours?" What rumours?"

He searched her eyes, looking for any sign that would confirm his worst fears. Afolabi paused, choosing his words carefully. He had tried to ignore the whispers, but the murmurs had grown louder, evolving into conversations that seemed to follow him everywhere.

"Yetunde," he began, his voice steady but edged with concern, "it's not just idle talk anymore. People are openly discussing your relationship with that with that guy at ASDA—Olakunle, or whatever you call his name. It's not just a rumour; everyone's noticing how much time you spend together, even at the car park."

The tension in the room became nearly unbearable, with unspoken words hanging between them. She opened her mouth, struggling to find a response, but the weight of her actions stilled her. Momentarily taken aback, she quickly shifted to a defensive tone. "Afolabi, you know how people love to talk," she said, her voice firm yet slightly raspy, betraying her uneasiness. "Olakunle is just a friend. Yes, we've run into each other a few times, but there's nothing more to it," she insisted, attempting to mask her discomfort with a show of strength confidence.

He was willing to trust her. He looked deeply into her eyes, hoping to find the truth and some comfort that could ease the turbulence within him. "I have faith in you, Yetunde," he said, his voice slightly trembling. "However, it can be quite challenging to avoid feeling concerned when those around me consistently amplify my uncertainties. I truly don't want to jeopardise what we have built; we have come a long way Yetunde."

Yetunde's expression softened as she gently reached out, clasping his hand in hers. "Afolabi, you must trust me. We're in this together, building our family's life and future. I would never do anything to put that at risk," she reassured, though her words lacked conviction. She subtly shifted her gaze away from his, concentrating on scratching a nonexistent itchy spot on her left knee.

He gently held her hand, seeking solace in their connection, yet uncertainties persisted, unyielding in their presence. He softly murmured his desire for everything to be alright, speaking more to himself than to her.

Her grasp tightened as if she was desperately trying to keep him by her side. "We will be, Afolabi." We must remain resilient and united."

Afolabi nodded, feeling a glimmer of hope, even as a lingering uncertainty tightened in his chest. Her words were all he had to hold onto, but as he looked into her eyes, he wondered if their love could withstand the weight of what lay unspoken between them. For now, he chose to believe, holding onto her hand as though it was the last thing tethering them to the life they'd shared. But in his heart, he knew they were walking on fragile ground, and every step felt like it might crack the foundation they had once built so confidently together.

As the days turned into weeks, Afolabi began to observe Yetunde more closely. Her occasional flattering reassurances were soothing, yet he could not shake the unsettling feeling that weighed heavily on his chest. However, he was aware of the damage to their trust and understood that repairing their relationship would require more than mere words.

The night was calm and peaceful, the kind of silence that amplified every little sound in the house. Afolabi sat on the edge of the bed, staring into the abyss of darkness. The twins were tucked into their beds, and the restlessness of the house was filled with the sound of their gentle breathing. For a moment, he wished life could be as easy for him as it was for his girls, who had nothing to worry about. He recalled how alert they had been, their beautiful, bright black eyes shining like diamonds as they listened to the story he had promised them earlier.

"The elephant planted okra in his garden, buffalo planted *shokoyokoto*, and ram planted garden eggs…" He was still in this introductory stage when the girls fell asleep. So, he tucked them neatly under their blankets.

His mind was filled with commotion, preoccupied by the widening gap between him and Yetunde. He had noticed the subtle shifts, small things he had previously overlooked: late-night text message notifications, her occasional distracted demeanour, her insistence on taking extra shifts, and her growing obsession with her phone. Each instance, though minor on its own, contributed to his increasing unease. He tried to dismiss it, attributing it to the stresses of work and the responsibilities of being a parent, but the uncomfortable feeling still clutched at his heart.

Afolabi was taken aback by the sudden ringing of his phone, which shattered the peaceful silence. He swiftly picked it up, careful not to disturb the sleeping girls. The name on the screen caused him a moment of hesitation. "Thomas." His former colleague from the care home. "Thomas, my man, how are you?" Afolabi inquired, trying to maintain a composed tone. "Ah, Afolabi, good evening. I apologise for reaching out at this hour," Thomas replied, his casual tone hinting at something that made Afolabi's heart race. "I wanted to check on you since it has been quite some time since our last conversation.

Afolabi let out a sigh of relief. "No problem, my friend. How's your job going? It's just another hectic night, I presume."

Thomas let out a small laugh. "Yeah, nothing new or exciting. I always enjoy it whenever I book overtime for the night; it's less hectic. Yet, another endless night. *You know, say, Naija people talk say anywhere wey belle face, na there be front.* But let's shift the focus away from myself; how's the new job going for you?"

They had a brief conversation about work, with Afolabi discussing the challenges and successes of his new IT position. It was pleasant to catch up, but as the conversation began to wind down, Thomas' disposition changed.

"So, I hope Yetunde is having a great evening away from work?" Thomas asked casually, but

Afolabi sensed a hint of curiosity that made him uneasy.

"Away from work?" Afolabi responded, his grip on the phone tightening. "She's actually at work."

There was a long pause on the other end of the phone, a heavy silence that seemed to stretch between them. When Thomas finally spoke, his voice was tentative, almost uncertain, as if he were weighing each word. "Well, that's... odd," he said slowly. "I'm working tonight, too, and I haven't seen her anywhere. Not once. It's strange, really—she's always around, but tonight... nothing." His words trailed off; the unease palpable in his tone.

Afolabi felt a sudden rush of anxiety, his heart pounding in his chest. "Maybe she's in a different part of the building or taking a break," he said, trying to sound nonchalant but unable to mask the anxiety in his voice

"Hmm," Thomas replied, still not entirely convinced. "Perhaps. However, I have spent quite a lot of time in this place, and it is common for our paths to cross at some point during the night. I found it rather strange, not even during the handover." His words lingered in the air, a quiet unease seeping into his tone. It was as if he was attempting to make sense of something that didn't quite add up, something that felt off, but he could not quite pinpoint it.

Afolabi's chest tightened and his throat swelled, his thoughts spinning. "Yeah, it is strange," he remarked, trying to keep a casual tone. "However, I'm confident there must be a valid explanation. Thanks for letting me know," Thomas".

They exchanged a few more pleasantries before the call ended, but Afolabi's mind refused to let go of the conversation. His hands, now trembling, betrayed the quiet panic building inside him. He gently placed the phone down, letting out a shaky breath, the weight of the moment settling heavily on his chest. His gaze drifted to the screen in front of him, but his thoughts were elsewhere—replaying Thomas' words over and over like a broken record.

"Yetunde... Absent from work?"

The phrase echoed in his mind. He could not shake the thought, his mind buzzing with endless possibilities. "Where could she be if not at the care home? And what possible reason would she have to lie?" An unsettling sensation curled in his gut, the kind that always appeared when doubt began to creep in. He tried to piece together the fragments of his concerns, but the doubts only seemed to multiply, casting a shadow over his thoughts.

Afolabi longed to trust her, to hold on to the faith he had always placed in Yetunde—the woman who had been his partner, his confidant, the one with whom he had shared his deepest fears and hopes. But the uncertainty that had once been a small flash of suspicion had now rooted itself deep within him, growing and fed by every inconsistency and every unanswered question. The more he thought about it, the more the feeling of unease began to consume him. It was no longer a fleeting doubt; it was a presence, one that seemed to demand his immediate attention.

As he pondered the matter further, a growing sense of unease washed over him. He could no longer ignore Thomas' words, realising they were more than mere coincidences. A more profound truth demanded his attention, a truth he could not ignore. What if Thomas was wrong? The thought surfaced, but it did little to ease his troubled mind. What if there was a perfectly reasonable explanation for her absence tonight? A plausible excuse, something he had not considered?" He tried to hold on to that possibility, tried to quiet the growing sense of dread. But it was harder than it should have been. The nagging thought that there might not be a logical explanation at all unsettled him further. "What if this was more than just a coincidence?"

The question hung in the air like a heavy fog. "How could I even bring this up?" He wondered aloud, his voice distant, almost unfamiliar, as though it belonged to someone else entirely. The idea of confronting Yetunde with the possibility of deceit—or worse, betrayal—felt wrong, deeply unsettling. A part of him recoiled from the very thought. And yet, he could no longer ignore Thomas' words. They lingered, pressing on him as if they held the key to something far deeper, something he wasn't ready to face.

With a quiet groan, Afolabi dropped his head into his hands, wrestling with the turmoil inside him. What am I supposed to do? He could no longer deny the weight of his doubts nor the quiet suspicion troubling his conscience. Every instinct told him something wasn't right—but how could he uncover the truth without tearing everything apart? The questions that had seemed like mere fragments moments ago had now become an inescapable web, pulling him deeper into uncertainty.

Sleep slipped away from him like water through his fingers, leaving him restless and wide-eyed in the dark. His thoughts churned, relentless and insistent. Answers. He needed answers. He glanced at the clock, noting it was a little after midnight. Yetunde still had a few hours before she was due back from work, although the word itself now felt hollow in his mind, laced with doubt.

He considered calling her, reaching out to hear her voice, to hear her explanation, but the thought paralysed him. What could he possibly say? What words could he find that would not sound accusatory, that would not betray the troubling suspicion in his chest? He could not bear the idea of sounding paranoid or distrustful. He loved her, yet here he was, wrestling with shadows of doubt. His mind spiralled, weighing how to approach her, his thoughts a kaleidoscope of possibilities—each one darker, more unsettling than the last.

He took a deep breath, trying to steady himself and gather some semblance of control. In the end, he chose to wait. Time. He would wait. His heart was a frantic rhythm in his chest, a mix of apprehension and resolve. He could not ignore it any longer—he had to uncover the truth. He needed to understand why Yetunde had not been at the care home that night, why she had missed their handover, and why she was not answering his growing suspicions. But more than that, he needed to comprehend what was happening to them—to their marriage. The slow unravelling of the bond they had once shared, the erosion of the trust he thought unshakable.

As the minutes bled into hours as Afolabi found himself sinking deeper into the ocean of his thoughts.

His mind swirled with chaotic fragments—memories of their happier moments, of laughter shared over quiet dinners, of intimate instances that now seemed so distant. He clung to the hope that he was wrong, that when Yetunde walked in through that door, there would be a simple, straightforward explanation—one that would restore his peace and his trust.

But deep down, he could feel it. A growing certainty that this night—this very moment—would be a turning point, a fork in the road. The kind that could either reunite them if the pieces fell back into place or push them further apart if the truth was more than he was prepared to face. And though part of him wished he could put it off, pretending everything was fine, the other part knew there was no going back now. This would define them, one way or another.

Afolabi found himself glancing at the clock every few minutes, mentally calculating how much time remained until Yetunde would return. Each tick of the second hand felt like an eternity. He attempted to immerse himself in the book he had been reading earlier, but the words blurred together, their meaning lost amid the rising tide of anxiety that seemed to have taken over every corner of his mind.

Then, at long last, the sound of keys in the lock reached his ears, followed by the faint creak of the front door swinging open. His pulse quickened. Yetunde stepped into the room. Afolabi studied her intently, his gaze sharp, searching for any hint or subtle shift in her demeanour that might reveal something he hadn't noticed before.

But Yetunde moved with the same ease, placing her bag on the table and kicking off her shoes as if everything were normal. She gave him a small, weary smile, the same one she always wore at the end of a long night, the kind that spoke of exhaustion but also of resilience.

"Had a busy night?" Afolabi enquired, his voice tight, betraying a hint of the tension simmering beneath the surface.

She nodded, letting out a soft, almost inaudible sigh. "Indeed. Quite so. I'm completely worn out."

Afolabi hesitated, the words he had rehearsed in his mind now trapped in his throat. Should he confront her now? Should he ask about her absence from work or the strange things Thomas had said? Doubt plagued him, but so did the fear that perhaps he was reading too much into things. What if this was all a misunderstanding? What if there was a perfectly logical explanation, and his questions only served to drive a wedge between them?

"Why don't you take a seat?" he suggested,

forcing a smile. "I'll prepare a cup of tea for you." Yetunde was surprised by the offer but did not decline. "I would greatly appreciate that, thank you."

As he unplugged the kettle, a surge of conflicting thoughts rushed through him, as if the disconnection between the appliances mirrored the growing distance between them. He wanted to believe in her and tell himself that Thomas was lying. But the doubt remained, and it felt like the connection between them had been switched off, like the unplugged kettle now silent and powerless.

As he passed her the cup of tea, their fingers lightly touched, evoking a fleeting sense of connection—a gentle reminder of the love that had united them. However, the burden of unexpressed anxieties and the grip of uncertainty cast a shadow over his thoughts. They sat in silence, sipping their tea; the familiar calm they once enjoyed was now replaced by an atmosphere of unease and fragility. Afolabi observed Yetunde discreetly, attempting to decode her thoughts and find any signs of reassurance in her behaviour. Yetunde remained as composed as ever, her expression closed off, concealing whatever thoughts lay beneath the surface. He felt the distance widening, the gap between the woman he had loved and the stranger sitting before him.

The silence was suffocating, the tension palpable. He could not ignore the insomnia that had been steadily creeping up on him, the sleepless nights that had become all too familiar. And, as if on cue, the anxiety that had been churning in his mind took root in his body, weighing heavily on his head. He knew he could not afford to be late for work—not in his line of work, not with the stakes so high. One mistake, one slip-up, and his job could be at risk. With a quiet sigh, he excused himself and forced himself into motion. His legs carried him through the motions as he hurriedly prepared for work, aware he had an important meeting that day at the office.

As he left for work, his anxiety did not ease. If anything, it only intensified, swelling into a quiet determination he could not ignore. He knew one thing for sure now: he could not keep living like this, trapped in a constant state of doubt and fear, unsure of where things were headed or what was true anymore. He had to know the truth. No matter what it would take, he was resolved to uncover it.

For the time being, though, he could only wait. He could only hope that Yetunde was still the woman he had trusted, that the distance between them was temporary, and that his doubts would prove to be nothing more than the product of a restless mind. Afolabi sensed that this was just the beginning and that their path was unclear. The trust that had once been the foundation of their marriage now felt fragile, and he feared the repercussions if it were to break.

He was plagued by these thoughts throughout the day, causing him to lose concentration every now and then while he worked. As the evening progressed, Afolabi's anxiety persisted. If anything, it intensified, becoming a determination that he could not overlook. He realised he could not continue living in such a state—overwhelmed by uncertainty and beset by constant doubt. He was resolute in uncovering the truth, irrespective of what it may be. For the time being, he decided to be patient and prayed that Yetunde remained the woman he had known trusted.

On his way back home, he resolved to confront the issue directly. As they sat together in the quiet of their home, the distance between them felt vast, causing Afolabi to wonder if they would ever rekindle their connection.

"Yetunde," his voice faltered as he called her name. "Where were you last night?" Yetunde looked at him, her brow furrowed with concern. "I was at work, of course. Why?"

Afolabi took a deep breath, his hands shaking slightly. "Thomas called. He said you weren't there."

Yetunde's eyes flickered with surprise before narrowing defensively. "So, it was him…" She thought. She remembered the shadowy figure—a man who had stood there for a brief moment, watching her. His presence, fleeting yet intense, had only briefly registered before he walked away. He must have been attracted by her excited moans. She did not take it to heart at that moment; after all, others were enjoying the same fun. Was it not a free society? It was only when Yetunde and Olakunle realised that being inside the car was no longer safe—that they were no longer alone-that they decided to leave the car park for Olakunle's house, where she spent the night.

But now, in the sharp light of Afolabi's accusation, the memory came rushing back, and the weight of her actions bore down on her like a crushing burden. Her voice hardened, becoming defensive, almost dismissive. "Thomas doesn't know what he's talking about. I was there."

"Don't lie to me, Yetunde!" Afolabi's voice rose, frustration seeping through. "I trusted you!" The words struck her like a physical blow. She flinched but only for a moment. Then, her eyes blazed with fury, her voice cutting like glass. "How dare you question me like this?" she snapped, her tone icy and sharp. "How I choose to spend my time is none of your business."

Afolabi felt a pang in his chest, a mixture of hurt, disbelief, and betrayal. His voice wavered, but the pain was evident. "It's my business when it affects our family. What's going on, Yetunde? Is this you... or someone else?" The question hung in the air, heavy with accusation.

Yetunde's eyes blazed with a sudden fury as she shot back, the question feeling like an insult, an attack on her very sense of autonomy. "Why are you questioning me in such a manner? I am your wife! Why won't you trust me? Her voice didn't tremble with vulnerability but with indignation. The deflection was instinctive, a protective reflex, but there was no guilt behind it— only a fierce desire to defend her actions.

"I have faith in you, Yetunde. However, you're not providing any substantial information. How can I stop worrying when you're being so mysterious?" Afolabi's voice was growing louder, not out of anger but from strain; every word was heavy with the weight of his fear and uncertainty.

She rose suddenly, her posture defensive, her stance almost militant. "How I choose to spend my time is my personal business, Afolabi. I don't owe you a detailed account of my daily activities." Her words were deliberate and cold, as if she were trying to assert control over the spiralling conversation.

Afolabi was overwhelmed by a deep sense of sadness and astonishment. The air between them had thickened, charged with unspoken emotions. He tried to steady his voice, but it trembled under the weight of his words. "It is my business when it impacts our family," he replied, his voice barely above a whisper. "I have the right to know what is happening. We can overcome this, Yetunde. We can face this together.

"Her determination was steadfast, like an impenetrable fortress. "There's no need for any adjustments, because everything is perfectly fine," she retorted sharply, her piercing voice slicing through the atmosphere precision.

The disagreement intensified, their words becoming increasingly cutting and hurtful until they both fell into a tense silence, burdened by the unspoken emotions lingering in the air. Afolabi sensed the growing divide as their once solid foundation of trust began to crumble amidst their uncertainties and allegations.

That night, Afolabi slept on the couch, staring at the ceiling, and replaying their conversation over and over in his mind. Where had it all gone wrong? he kept asking himself. How had they ended up on opposite sides of a widening chasm? The more he thought about it, the more he felt the distance between them grow, an invisible rift that seemed impossible to ignore.

He drifted in and out of a restless sleep, haunted by the uncertainty of their relationship and the fear that things might never be the same again. Each time he closed his eyes, a fresh wave of doubt would wash over him, leaving him wide awake once more, staring into darkness.

The next morning, Afolabi picked up his phone and called his sister, Bolanle, who had sponsored their relocation to the UK. As he explained his situation, she was boiling with anger, judging by the tone of her voice, out of concern for him.

"Afolabi, this cannot continue. You should address the situation as soon as possible before it gets out of hand. She ought to provide you with an explanation of where she was last night."

"I've done my best, Sister mi," Afolabi responded wearily. "But she refuses to engage with me."

"Then you should consider being more assertive. Don't allow her to distance herself from you. You're her husband; she should show some respect for you."

Afolabi let out a heavy sigh, burdened by the weight of his sister's words. "I don't want to pressure her", Sister mi. "I simply want to understand what is going on".

"Understanding is indeed very important. However, it is also essential to assert yourself and protect your loved ones. Don't let this break you down. One more thing, consider investigating some of these rumours to ascertain the actual truth."

"Thanks, Sister mi," he said quietly, his voice thick with emotion. "I'll do it. I'll talk to her." After the call ended, Afolabi sat in the silence of the room, tension still heavy in his chest. Bolanle's words echoed in his mind. "You deserve the truth." But what would the truth be? Would he be able to face it? And, more importantly, would Yetunde be honest with him? He did not know the answers, but one thing was certain—he could not keep living like this. The uncertainty, the doubt—it was consuming him alive.

With a deep sigh, he stood up with great determination to speak to her; whatever happened, he would confront it. The choice was no longer about remaining in the dark. It was about facing whatever the light might reveal.

As the day progressed, Yetunde received a call from Bolanle. The conversation quickly intensified.

"Yetunde, what have you been up to lately?" Bolanle inquired authoritatively.

Yetunde's anger ignited. "This is a private matter between husband and wife", she snapped, her voice growing colder by the second; "stay out of it".

Bolanle did not flinch. "Really, so it wasn't a private matter when I coughed up several thousand British pounds to sponsor your relocation to the UK!" she shot back, her words dripping with frustration and resentment. The accusation felt like a slap to Yetunde's face—one that stung far more than she was willing to admit.

Yetunde's pride surged, a wave of defiance filling her chest. With a tight, measured breath, she ended the call abruptly, her fingers trembling slightly as she pressed the red button. Her heart pounded, the anger and frustration swirling in her chest like a storm. Bolanle had no right to question her, no right to interfere. This was not about money, or their relocation, or anything else. This was her life, her marriage.

As she ended the call, a sense of dread crept in, like the calm before a storm. The walls in their home felt suddenly suffocating, the silence between her and

Afolabi louder than ever. She had tried to distance herself from him, to keep her emotions guarded, but it seemed every day brought a new battle. She could feel the tension in the air, thick and heavy, as though it were suffocating them both. Back in the living room, Afolabi was pacing. His mind was still reeling from the conversation with his sister, and the weight of his next steps pressed down on him. He knew Yetunde would be furious when she found out. But he had hoped—naively—that things could be salvaged if he had someone else to talk to, someone who cared about him and would see things clearly.

The door swung open, and Yetunde stepped into the room, her eyes narrowed and her posture rigid with barely concealed fury. A chill ran down Afolabi's spine as she glared at him, her expression contorted into something he'd never seen before, like a wounded lioness.

"So, you had the audacity to report me to your sister, Afolabi?" she hissed, her voice low and venomous, each word laced with contempt. Her gaze was cold, and the scowl on her face was so fierce that Afolabi could barely recognise her. This was no longer the woman he had married, the woman he had once trusted completely

The anger in her eyes was sharp, cutting through the air between them like a blade. She took a step closer to him, and although the space between them was still wide, it felt as though an emotional gap had opened up. "We have just started," she spat, her voice carrying a dangerous edge. The words, full of venom, struck Afolabi harder than he expected.

His heart sank. The fear he had been trying to suppress rose again, sharper and more piercing this time. "Where was this coming from?" he thought. "What had come over her?"

Yetunde's entire demeanour was different now. A distance lingered in her eyes—a coldness that chilled him to the bone. He had never seen her like this. This was not the woman he had once shared his life with. This was someone else, someone who appeared to resent his very presence as though the mere fact of his concern was an unforgivable sin.

Afolabi opened his mouth, trying to find the right words, but nothing emerged. His thoughts were too jumbled, too filled with the tension and betrayal he had experienced over the past few days. "Had he done something wrong by reaching out to Bolanle? Was that the breaking point?"

Yetunde's glare was unrelenting, and with every passing second, the distance between them seemed to grow. He could feel her pulling away but did not know how to stop it. Every word he had spoken in the past few days had only seemed to drive them further apart, and now, he could feel her slipping through his fingers.

"Yetunde," he finally managed, his voice rough, betraying the mix of hurt and confusion.

"Please… we need to talk. About everything. I don't want to fight like this."

She scoffed; the sound was bitter. "Talk? About what, exactly? You've already made your choice, Afolabi. You've chosen your side."

Her words stung, but there was nothing he could say to change them, nothing that could bridge the gap between them now. The silence that followed was thick with unresolved emotions, and Afolabi realised with a sinking feeling that this moment was only the beginning of something much worse. The cracks that had begun to appear in their relationship were now splintering wide open, and he was unsure how they could ever come back together.

Yetunde turned her back on him without another word, her steps heavy as she moved toward the bedroom. Afolabi stood motionless, the weight of her absence more suffocating than the words they had exchanged. He knew, with a crushing certainty, that whatever path they had been on before had now veered into uncertain, dangerous territory.

In the days that followed, Yetunde found herself bombarded with calls from Nigeria. Her parents urged her to resolve the conflict amicably.

"Yetunde," her mother's voice rang out through the phone, "your marriage is important. You should definitely have a conversation with your husband." Though her mother wasn't overly forceful, her words carried a gentle persistence, urging her to resolve any issues lingering between them. But Yetunde's pride was a wall she wasn't ready to tear down. "This is a private matter between Afolabi and me; stay out of it," she snapped, with an apparent finality in her tone.

"Yetunde, I am your mother; don't make the mistake of hanging up on me." As if she sensed what Yetunde was about to do.

"You may not know the value of what you have until you lose it," she continued. "You've been a great help to us ever since your marriage to this young man, even more so since your relocation. Remember this—no creeping plant ever makes it to the top without the support of a pole or standing tree, no matter how useless the tree or pole may be."

Yetunde remained defiant, her arrogance intensifying with each call. She was adamant about handling it in her own way, her voice sharp and distant.

Afolabi's mother began to consider whether paying them a visit to the UK could quench the crisis,

"Perhaps a visit to the UK might help resolve this. Besides, I'd like to see my son and

granddaughters," she said, glancing at her husband, whose face remained expressionless.

In response, Afolabi's father quietly picked up his tablet, initiated a video call with their son, and gestured for his wife to join him. As he adjusted the tablet, his face briefly twisted into a grimace before he quickly masked it. However, his wife's sharp eyes caught the fleeting expression, deepening her anxiety. She hurried over to sit beside him as he handed her the tablet.

"Good evening, Mum," Afolabi greeted when his mother's face appeared on the screen. His smile was polite, though the fatigue showed on his face was unmistakable.

"Good evening, my son. Are you feeling unwell?" she asked, her tone laced with concern.

"No, Mum. Why do you ask?" he replied, his voice laced with confusion.

"Your eyes—they look heavy and bloodshot. Talk to me, my son. I'm your mother," she urged anxiously.

Afolabi hesitated, scratching his head as he searched for the right words. "Mum, it's just… a combination of many things," he admitted, his voice trailing off.

"Like what?" she pressed, her voice gentle yet firm.

"The stress of work, and…" He paused, his throat tightening. "And some family issues. But Mum, you don't have to worry; I'm fine."

She did not buy it. "Why shouldn't I worry? You don't really know how you look. If it appears like

this on video, I wonder what it will be like in reality. In fact, I'm considering coming over to see you and my granddaughters."

"Mum, there's no need for that now," Afolabi said with emotion. "Just be praying for me, Mum." When Afolabi had finished talking with his mother, his father took back the tablet and removed his eyeglasses before looking back at the screen.

"Afolabi."

"Yes Dad."

"Did you tell your mother not to worry?" His father's voice was calm but carried a weight that made Afolabi feel even more unsettled.

"Yes, I did, Dad," Afolabi answered, his confusion mounting.

"Who needs that counsel?" His father's words hung heavily in the air. Afolabi gazed into his father's eyes and replied, "I understand," Dad."

"Only the living can make a difference," his father said, his voice stern and final. Without waiting for a response, he hung up the phone call.

Turning to his wife, Afolabi's father added, "Making a trip to the UK for this matter is out of the question. If she could hang up on Bolanle, would she treat you any differently? I think it's wiser not to allow for something that can't be reversed, regardless of the price paid later." Meanwhile, Afolabi became lost in thought, trying to connect his father's statement with their previous discussion. He felt trapped, unsure of how to move forward. His father's analogy about the clay pot and the stream echoed in his mind. It was the same approach of questioning and answering: "Afolabi, when one carries a large, heavy clay pot to the stream and fills it with water, does he need help to put it on his head?"

"He definitely does, Dad." He answered innocently.

"When his legs become wobbly and his hands tired from steadying the pot, what does he do?"

"He calls for help." Afolabi's curiosity picked at this point.

"And what if it's on a lonely path, what happens?"

"He stands the risk of…" The remaining words stuck to his throat as he realised what his father was driving at.

In the meantime, Pastor Adewale, their spiritual father, attempted to intervene, speaking with a sense of calm authority that Afolabi hoped might bridge the divide.

"Yetunde and Afolabi, as Christians, it is important for both of you to communicate and collaborate to resolve this. Your family's unity is dependent on it."

Afolabi was pleased to have the pastor's involvement, as he believed it could help bridge the widening gap. However, Yetunde maintained her emotional distance, keeping her walls up and preventing others from getting close.

As time passed, the tension in the household continued to escalate. Afolabi and Yetunde hardly exchanged words, their interactions filled with tension and discomfort. Their twins, Dara and Dami, could sense the friction and became more withdrawn, their usual bright smiles replaced with expressions of uncertainty. Afolabi could not help but feel that the rift between him and Yetunde was not just affecting their relationship—it was also affecting their children.

At night, when the house fell silent and the twins were fast asleep, Afolabi would sit alone in the dimly lit living room, his gaze fixed on the shadowy walls. The weight of it all bore down on him—loneliness, frustration, guilt—all tangled in a suffocating knot. Beneath it lay an unsettling fear, troubling him to the core. "Was it too late? Had the damage already become irreparable?"

The silence in the house seemed to grow louder with each passing day, and Afolabi knew that something had to change. But he did not know how. He did not know how to bridge the growing gap between him and Yetunde or how to bring back the lightness and laughter that had once filled their lives home.

For now, he clung to one thing: the hope that, with time, things would improve. That, somehow, they would find their way back to each other and to the family they had once been

One evening, after yet another quiet dinner, Afolabi decided to try to connect with Yetunde again.

"We really need to have a discussion about the current situation. This… this situation is unsustainable."

Yetunde looked at him with a cold, detached stare. "I don't have anything to say, Afolabi, just let it be," she replied, her tone dismissive.

Afolabi felt a wave of disappointment, but he remained determined. "This goes beyond just us, Yetunde," he pressed, his voice softening. "This is about our family. Dara and Dami need us both. They need our collective support."

Her demeanour softened momentarily, revealing a fleeting glimpse of the person he used to be acquainted with before she returned to her hardened state. "I need my space, Afolabi. Can you please give me some space?"

The words were a soft plea, yet the tone was anything but gentle. There was no room for discussion or negotiation in her request. The desire for space was more than a simple need for quiet; it was a signal that she was retreating further into herself, pushing him away in a way that made him feel like an outsider in his own home.

Afolabi's heart dropped. He had feared this, but hearing it spoken aloud was different-it was a stark acknowledgment that their marriage was no longer a partnership. It had become a series of isolated individuals living under the same roof, bound together by obligations but disconnected in every other form or sense.

He wanted to argue, to tell her that he needed answers too, that he could not keep living like this- wondering where they had gone wrong. But as he opened his mouth, the words seemed too heavy, too futile. It was as if the conversation they needed to have could no longer be found in the space between them.

"I'll give you space," he said quietly, the defeat in his voice unmistakable. He did not want to, but what else could he do? He had tried, for what felt like the thousandth time, to reach out to her, to cling to the fragments of what they had once shared. But all he got in return was a cold wall.

She nodded without a word, turning away as if he were no longer there, no longer important enough to acknowledge. The silence in the room grew unbearable, pressing against his chest like a weight.

Afolabi stood there a moment longer, his mind racing, his heart aching. He wanted to mend this, but he did not know how. He wanted to fight for their family, for the love they had built, but he was uncertain if she was still fighting alongside him.

And so, he left the room, the sound of his footsteps echoing in the hallway, the distance between them growing ever wider.

Over the weekend, Afolabi decided to take Dara and Dami to the park, hoping that the change of scenery would lift their spirits. The gentle hum of life around them—children laughing, the distant chirp of birds, and the rustling of leaves—felt like a fleeting distraction from the heaviness pressing down on his chest. But as he watched Dara and Dami running ahead, their laughter echoing in the crisp air, a profound sadness washed over him.

The sight of his children, so innocent and carefree, stirred something deep within. Their joy, so unburdened and pure, stood in stark contrast to the growing strain in his own heart. As Dara chased Dami around the playground, both of them shrieking with delight, Afolabi's heart ached. This was what he wanted for them: the happiness, the security, the warmth of a home filled with love.

Yet, something had shifted, and now he was uncertain how to return to that place.

His mind wandered back to Yetunde, contemplating the quiet distance that had grown too vast to ignore between them.

It was not just their marriage that was unravelling; it was the foundation they had built together, the promises they had made, and the future they had dreamed of. He could feel it slipping away, each day marking another fracture in the bond that had once seemed unbreakable.

A part of him wanted to reach out to Yetunde, to confront the unspoken distance between them once more. But as much as he longed to, he understood that forcing her into a conversation when she clearly was not ready would only make matters worse. He could not force her to feel something she was not ready to feel, nor could he force her to come to him on his terms. But still, the thought of losing her, of the disconnection between them becoming permanent, was unbearable.

As he sat on the bench, watching Dara and Dami climb and slide, he was struck by the stark reality of his situation. The family he had once dreamed of, the life he had worked so hard to build, was teetering on the edge. Was it too late to fix things? Was the rift between him and Yetunde something they could overcome, or was it already too wide to mend?

But watching the twins, so full of life, so full of promise, reminded him of what was at stake. He could not give up on this. He could not give up on them. He did not know precisely what the path forward looked like, but he knew that letting go was not an option. He had to be patient. He had to believe that with time, understanding, and a willingness to confront the truth, there was still a chance to find their way back to one another.

After a while, Dara and Dami finally grew weary. Sitting beside him on the bench with their ice creams, Afolabi felt a bittersweet pang in his chest. Their tiny hands, sticky with sugar, reached for him instinctively, drawing him back into the present. He smiled, though it did not quite reach his eyes.

"Are we ready to go home?" he asked softly, looking down at them.

Both nodded enthusiastically, their laughter and joy still infectious. As they walked back home, Afolabi's heart felt a bit lighter, but the questions lingered in the back of his mind. What was the next step? How could he bring the warmth back into his marriage? But for now, he would continue to fight—for them, his children, and the family he believed was still worth saving.

When they arrived home, Afolabi found Yetunde sitting on the sofa, engrossed in the television. He paused for a moment, then quietly sat beside her, hoping that this small gesture might help bridge the distance that had grown between them.

"Yetunde," he whispered gently, his voice filled with a mixture of desire and understanding. "I have strong feelings for you. I truly value our connection and am determined to maintain it. Let's collaborate to find a solution to this.

Yetunde turned to him, her gaze filled with disgust. "How dare you come and sit next to me?" she snapped; her voice heavy with frustration. I find it increasingly difficult to tolerate your presence these days, Afolabi. The smell and touch of you now irritate me."

With a final, resentful look, as if she was looking for the slightest opportunity, she abruptly stood up. She stormed out of the house, leaving Afolabi in shock, his heart heavy with the weight of her words and the uncharted waters ahead.

The front door slammed behind Yetunde with a finality that echoed through the house. Afolabi remained frozen on the couch, his chest heavy and his thoughts swirling in a disorienting fog. Her words, smell, and touch of you now irritate me, cutting deeper than any wound he had ever felt. He tried to reach out, fix things, and bring her back to a place where their connection had once meant something. But in that moment, it felt like all his efforts had been in vain.

Afolabi did not know how long he had sat there, trying to make sense of it all. His heart ached, yet amidst his pain, a strange clarity began to form. He had given Yetunde space and tried to provide her with the time she asked for, but now he realised he had failed to see how much the emotional gap had widened between them. He had assumed that time would heal; that their shared love for their children would keep them together, but something far more fundamental was missing—a deeper intimacy, a reconnection that neither of them had been willing to fight for.

He stood up, pacing slowly through the living room, his thoughts returning to the twins: Dara and Dami. What would this mean for them? He had hoped their family would be a place of peace and warmth, but it seemed as if everything was falling apart at that moment. The calm he had worked so hard to create was unraveling, and he could not find a way to fix it.

Outside, Yetunde leaned against the cold brick wall, her heart racing. The night air was refreshing, even as it failed to soothe the storm within her. Memories of Olakunle surged in her mind-each one a vivid reminder of the spark she had lost with Afolabi. With Olakunle, everything felt alive; even their spontaneous beach trip was electrifying, filled with laughter and thrilling kisses that reignited desires she thought were gone.

In contrast, Afolabi's love felt familiar and predictable. He was kind and respectful, but their lives had settled into a comfortable routine-dinner at home, watching television, and quiet evenings apart. Every attempt to rekindle the intimacy was met with doubt, leaving her feeling frustrated and unfulfilled.

Yetunde found herself yearning for excitement and adventure. Afolabi's steady love felt somewhat dull, while Olakunle celebrated her in ways that made her feel vibrant and alive. Every moment with Olakunle highlighted what she was missing: the shared laughter, not to mention the spark that had faded with Afolabi.

As she stood there, Yetunde felt the wetness between her thighs. Excitement stirred in her stomach; the pull of her connection with Olakunle was undeniable. With Afolabi, love felt like a steady and peaceful stream, while Olakunle was a wild, untamed river. Every moment with him awakened a longing within her, a yearning for the intensity and passion he brought-an experience unlike any other.

Should she cling to Afolabi's comforting routine, or embrace Olakunle's thrilling unpredictability? The decision weighed heavily on her mind. Yetunde recalled Afolabi's support and quiet strength, yet those memories dimmed in comparison to the vibrant experiences shared with Olakunle.

With a deep breath, Yetunde resolved to confront her truths. It was time to discover what she truly wanted for herself and both men. She needed to choose a path that honoured her desires. As she stepped into the night, the weight of uncertainty began to lift, and for the first time, she felt a spark of hope for a fresh start.

Chapter 10

The Struggle for Connection

The once lively home had transformed into a place of quietude and distance. Although Afolabi and Yetunde resided in the same house and slept in the same bed, their lives were marked by a noticeable separation. Yetunde's presence in the house was a stark contrast to the closeness they once shared. The formerly warm, shared spaces had grown cold and unwelcoming; each corner now highlighted the increasing distance between them.

Afolabi, determined to mend the growing divide, made multiple efforts to interact with Yetunde. He left notes on her pillow, hoping to initiate some form of communication. He attempted to prepare her favourite food, believing that the comfort of familiarity might alleviate the strain. Every gesture was met with either indifference or icy rejection. On the rare occasions they did talk, their conversations were brief and curt, usually about the children or household matters. There was no warmth in her voice, no spark in her eyes, and each attempt he made to reconnect was met with apathy. He had become accustomed to the silence that filled the house like an impenetrable barrier fog.

Afolabi tried to keep the twins as normal as possible by maintaining routines, helping with homework, telling them stories, and playing games with them. However, even with them, he could feel the absence of their usual family harmony—a nagging emptiness that lingered like a silent witness to their fractured relationship.

Bayo was taken aback when Afolabi opened up to him about the challenges he was facing. The change in his heart-shaped face was remarkable. He transitioned from astonishment to a deep sense of worry as he hung on to every word.

"I had no clue it was this bad," Bayo exclaimed, shaking his head in disbelief. "You mean you've been dealing with these all along?"

Afolabi sighed, his voice laced with a mix of relief and frustration. "It's been a challenge, Bayo; I feel like I'm running out of options."

Bayo paused for a moment, gathering his thoughts before replying. "You know, Afolabi, perhaps there is a solution to your predicament. Have you considered exploring job opportunities that offer sponsorship? It could potentially provide you with a more secure footing here in the UK."

Afolabi frowned, clearly expressing his doubt. "I understand your suggestion, Bayo, but I don't believe it will be necessary. I have complete faith in my wife and am confident we can work through this situation together. Yetunde wouldn't do anything to put my position at risk. We've been through so much together."

"I understand your perspective, Afolabi, and I can see why you have confidence in your wife," he said, his concern deepening. However, it may be wise to have an alternative strategy ready. What if things don't proceed as planned?" As he spoke, he nodded his head in sync with his words, and the keys in his hand also produced a corresponding sound as he fidgeted with them. This was his manner whenever he felt emotionally unsettled.

Afolabi shook his head, remaining steady. "I simply cannot envision it reaching that point. I have complete confidence that she will not engage in such devious behaviour. I'll figure this out on my own, and

I won't require any assistance with employment."

Bayo let out a weary sigh, hesitant to be too forceful yet troubled. "I hope you're right, Afolabi. However, it may be wise to consider alternative possibilities just to be safe. A new beginning awaits you, even if you might not perceive it at this moment."

Afolabi nodded reluctantly, although his doubts persisted. "I'll consider it, but I genuinely believe it won't be necessary. We'll make it" through."

Bayo mustered a smile, fully aware that persuading Afolabi was futile at that moment. "Okay, just remember that I'm here to support you. No matter what happens, we will find a solution as a team."

The silence between them grew particularly heavy one evening. Unsettled by the increasing strain in their relationship, Afolabi decided it was time to bridge the gap. He approached Yetunde in the kitchen, his voice calm but underscored by a subtle vulnerability

"Yetunde," he said softly, his voice steady yet carrying a vulnerable tremor. "Can we talk? I am eager to better understand the situation and explore potential solutions."

Yetunde's response was quick and harsh. Her gaze turned focused; her tone icy. "If you keep pestering me, I will call the police for you for pressuring and stressing me out."

A sudden, sickening chill washed over Afolabi. His pulse quickened, and for a moment, the world seemed to narrow down to just her words echoing in his mind. "Threatening him with the police? What? Has it really come to this, Yetunde?" he stammered, his voice barely above a whisper, the sting of disbelief intertwined with pain. "You mean you would go that far?"

Tears welled up in his eyes as he sank to his knees, the weight of their unravelling marriage crashing down on him like an avalanche. He reached out a trembling hand toward her. "Yetunde, please." Consider Dara and Dami. Let's not allow anger and resentment to tear our family apart. Don't let yourself be manipulated in this way."

Yetunde's gaze remained firm, her expression as chilly as the November wind. With a final indifferent look, she spun around and strode off, leaving Afolabi alone on the cold kitchen floor. The door slammed shut behind her, leaving him kneeling in the kitchen. Her words weighed heavily on him, their stark truth piercing his heart with an icy sting as his outstretched hand hung in the air, a desperate gesture to reclaim something that now felt so distant

Days passed, and the silence became overwhelming. Afolabi immersed himself in his work, seeking solace through the power of distraction. However, even amid his busy work life, his thoughts were constantly drawn back to the breakdown of his marriage. Every corner of the house, every echo of Yetunde's footsteps, taunted his large heart with longing for what had been taken away.

Yetunde's demeanour grew more confrontational. She rejected any attempts at closeness, her body language exuding defiance. She distanced herself from his touch and turned down his advances in bed, leaving him to struggle with the ensuing rejection. Her icy demeanour extended beyond her emotions, creating a seemingly impassable barrier.

On one particularly cold evening, as the first frost of winter settled over London, Afolabi found himself alone in the bedroom he had once shared with Yetunde. The bed, now a battleground of unspoken words and unresolved issues, seemed to amplify their silence. Yetunde's absence troubled him, steadily eroding the fragile remnants of hope he had once clung to. He lay there, staring at the ceiling, the weight of their separation pressing heavily upon his chest.

The room, which had once been filled with hope and shared dreams, now felt empty, almost as if the bed had grown in length and width, swallowing him whole in its vast, lonely expanse. Meanwhile, Yetunde's actions became increasingly unpredictable. She began spending more time outside the house, using excuses like "urgent errands" or "late shifts" at the care home. Her frequent and unexplained absences left Afolabi feeling ever more insecure. Her phone calls and texts were frequently brief and unsympathetic, offering minimal reassurance or clarification. The once-familiar routine of their life together had fallen apart, leaving behind a collection of isolated and disconnected moments.

One evening, Afolabi decided to approach Yetunde once more in hopes of gaining a clearer understanding of the situation. She had finally returned home after being away for three days without any notice or phone call. As she entered the room, Afolabi approached her, his voice filled with urgency yet composed. "Yetunde, what has become of you? You are rarely present, and when you are, you seem emotionally distant. I'm feeling overwhelmed."

Yetunde's anger boiled over. "What do you want from me, Afolabi? I'm doing my best to handle everything. You're not making this any easier for me."

Without a word, she turned and stormed off to the bedroom, slamming the door with such force that it rattled the walls. The impact sent their wedding picture tumbling from the living room wall, shattering the glass frame as it hit the floor. Afolabi flinched at the sound, his heart sinking as he stared at the fragments scattered across the room. He beckoned the twins to remain in their room as he bent down to pick up the picture, his fingers trembling as they brushed against the shards. The image beneath the cracked glass captured a moment from a different life—a younger, happier version of them, glowing with love as they exchanged vows on a sunlit day. He could still remember the warmth of her smile, the light in her eyes, and the quiet promise they had made to stand by each other through everything.

Now, that promise felt as fragile as the broken frame. Afolabi stood there, the photograph clutched in his hand, his chest tight with the weight of their unravelling. The sound of her door slamming reverberated in his mind, a painful reminder of how far they had drifted apart. The distance between them felt insurmountable, like an endless void that grew wider with every argument and every unspoken word. He longed to step closer, to reach out, but he did not know where to begin—or if she even wanted him to try.

As he swept the shards of glass into a dustpan, tears flowed down his cheeks as his thoughts lingered on their wedding day. The memory seemed almost surreal now, like a cherished dream he could not quite grasp. He remembered her laughter ringing out as they danced, her hand warm in his, the world around them blurring as they promised to build a future together. But now, as he straightened and looked again at the cracked picture, he could not help but wonder if that future had slipped away, shattered like the glass at his feet.

Weeks turned into months, and the cracks in their marriage deepened. Afolabi found solace in the fleeting moments of normalcy with Dara and Dami. He made it a priority to be an involved father, doing his utmost to shield his children from the constant conflicts that affected his household. Their laughter, although less frequent, offered comfort to his weary spirit. He took them to the park now and then, shared bedtime stories with them, and cherished the brief moments of happiness that reminded him of the family he was determined to preserve.

The atmosphere in the household grew increasingly tense, weighing heavily on Afolabi. Despite his best efforts, the distance between them seemed to widen. Afolabi's heart was troubled by a blend of optimism and acceptance as he navigated the difficult terrain of a broken connection. The future appeared uncertain, yet he persevered for the sake of his loved ones, clinging to the fragile hope that, somehow, they might still find a way to mend their relationship relationships.

Over the weekend, Afolabi decided to take Dara and Dami to a nearby park, hoping that a change of scenery would lift their spirits. The crisp air and the sight of children playing brought a sense of normalcy and happiness that had been missing from their lives. He watched his daughters joyfully darting about, their laughter breaking through the heavy stillness that had engulfed them.

As he gently pushed Dara on the swing, Afolabi's mind drifted back to Yetunde. He pondered the path they had taken to reach this point and questioned why their once unbreakable connection now seemed so fragile. Every sway back and forth and every burst of laughter from his daughters served as a poignant reminder of the deep affection and harmony that had once characterised their family. However, as time passed, it became increasingly difficult to maintain that sense of unity. Later that evening, after a peaceful dinner with Dara and Dami, they jumped on him and demanded,

"Daddy, tell us that story again!"

"Which one of them? I've told you so many stories." He asked with a smile.

"The giant white wicked bird!" They chorused.

He looked into their starry eyes and said, "Sure you won't sleep midway?" They shook their heads vigorously and said, "No, Daddy!"

OK, let's continue. Three of them were very strong and lived together with their mother, who prepared delicious meals for them using vegetables from their garden. However, one day she went to the garden and discovered that all the vegetables had already been harvested. So ...

At this point, the girls had already fallen fast asleep on his body. He gently lifted them to their room, carefully laid them on the bed, and covered them with blankets.

Afolabi found himself alone in the living room, gazing at the empty spot where Yetunde used to be. He revisited the numerous conversations and arguments they had engaged in, desperately seeking a hint, a pivotal moment that could have altered the course of events. The stillness was overwhelming, interrupted only by the steady rhythm of the clock-a constant reminder of the unstoppable march of time and the lingering unease that permeated every inch of their surroundings.

Yetunde's prolonged absences became more frequent. She seemed to be spending less time at home, often returning late and appearing distracted. Afolabi grew increasingly concerned as he struggled to understand her actions.

After a late night out, Yetunde returned home to find Afolabi trying to reach out to her once more. He stood in the doorway of their room, speaking with a gentle yet sincere tone.

"Yetunde, we need to talk." I have concerns about you and our relationship. We cannot continue like this; this is not what we originally planned when relocating to the UK.

Yetunde barely looked away from her phone, her face showing signs of fatigue. "I've had a really long and intense night out, Afolabi. Is it possible to address this matter tomorrow?

"No, it cannot," Afolabi insisted, his voice filled with desperation. "It seems that our connection with one another is slipping away. I want you to shed light on what is actually happening."

She sighed deeply, clearly expressing her frustration through her body language. "I'm giving it my all." I can't fulfil everyone's expectations at the expense of my well-being."

The conversation concluded with Yetunde seeking solace in her personal haven, leaving Afolabi to grapple with his growing concerns. The distance between them appeared insurmountable, and every attempt at communication only seemed to exacerbate matters, deepening the divide that had formed.

One afternoon, Afolabi received a call from Pastor Adewale, who had been trying to mediate between them. The pastor's voice was calm and comforting, offering solace to Afolabi's weary spirit.

"Afolabi, I've spoken with Yetunde." She's facing numerous challenges that are significantly affecting your relationship. It's crucial to approach this situation with patience and empathy."

Afolabi nodded. "I'm doing my best, Pastor." However, it can be challenging when communication feels one-sided. Yetunde seems uninterested in engaging in any conversation."

"Patience is vital," Pastor Adewale advised gently. "Remember to maintain a balance between reaching out to others and prioritising your own well-being. Yetunde's heart cannot be changed by one person alone; it requires effort from both parties. More importantly, you need to involve God. Therefore, you must be fervent in prayer during this difficult time."

Afolabi deeply pondered the pastor's words, even as he grappled with increasing frustration. He remained dedicated to his work and his children, steadfast in his commitment to creating a secure and nurturing atmosphere for them, even amidst the chaos within their household.

However, every encounter with Yetunde served as a constant reminder of the affection that appeared to have diminished, substituted by a distant and steady quietness.

Afolabi found the nights to be the most challenging. He lay in bed, gazing at the ceiling, deep in contemplation. The pain of Yetunde's absence was intensified by the realisation that they had once shared a strong connection that now felt distant. Every day presented Afolabi with a fresh obstacle, and he held onto the belief that, despite the chaos, there could still be a way to find common ground.

As time passed, Afolabi and Yetunde's home became a place of constant tension, with emotions running high and words left unsaid. The laughter of Dara and Dami served as a poignant reminder of the severity of the situation. Despite the growing separation, Afolabi's devotion to his family never wavered. He understood that the journey towards reconciliation would be arduous and fraught with obstacles. Nevertheless, he made a firm decision to persevere, holding onto the hope that, in some miraculous manner, they would reunite.

Chapter 11

The Final Blow

The late afternoon sun streamed through the window, casting a soft, melancholic glow over the room as Afolabi entered, struggling to carry his load of groceries. The peaceful stillness of the house was broken by the unexpected sight of a brown envelope on the kitchen counter. His pulse quickened as his eyes fixed on the emblem of the Home Office, the bold stamp daring him to confront what lay inside. Strictly Confidential: To the Addressee Only—the words seemed to echo in the silence, a weight settling in his stomach.

With a mix of anticipation and nerves, he dropped the bags in his hands, carefully tore open the envelope, and removed the letter. The words burst forth from the page, every sentence piercing his heart like a sharp blade. Yetunde had indeed cancelled his dependent visa. The letter gave him 60 days to get a Certificate of Sponsorship or leave the UK—an ultimatum that felt like a harsh turn of events.

He slumped into the chair in the kitchen, feeling as if the world was crumbling around him, overwhelmed by the magnitude of the situation. Emotion overcame him, and tears filled his eyes. His grip on the letter tightened as though it held the weight of the world.

"Ye! Ye!! Ye!! Yetunde ti pa mi oo, she has killed me! How could she do this?" Afolabi whispered, his voice thick with anguish, barely a breath above a sob. The stillness of the room echoed his pain, the silence now a stark contrast to the life and laughter that had once filled these walls. The kitchen, once a place of comfort, felt suddenly suffocating; its familiar warmth turned cold as he stared at the letter in his hands. The words blurred before his eyes, their cruel meaning sinking deeper with every passing second, as if their weight might crush him where he stood.

That evening, Yetunde returned home, her footsteps unusually light, as if she anticipated a difficult conversation. She glanced at Afolabi, who sat on the couch in the living room, his face hidden behind his hands. The atmosphere was thick with intensity.

Afolabi's voice trembled as he lifted his gaze, his

eyes searching hers with a mix of pain and disbelief. "Yetunde... why?" he asked, his voice barely above a whisper. "Why did you cancel my visa? This... this is an unforgivable betrayal." The words hung in the air between them, heavy with the weight of unanswered questions, the silence stretching out as he waited for an explanation that seemed impossible to find.

Yetunde's expression remained indifferent, her gaze steady and devoid of emotion. She stood there for a long moment as though weighing her words carefully before finally speaking. "I made the best decision for me and my children," she said flatly. "This marriage... it's just not working." The finality in her tone left no room for negotiation, her words cutting through the air like a cold wind. Afolabi's heart sank as the weight of her words settled in, each syllable deeper and more incomprehensible than the last.

Afolabi felt a deep sense of disappointment upon hearing her words. "Is this the best option for the children?" It seems that their family is finally being torn apart. "How can this be most beneficial for them?"

"They'll come to understand eventually," Yetunde replied nonchalantly, shrugging off the matter. "It would be in everyone's best interest if you left."

Afolabi's eyes brimmed with tears as he

struggled to maintain his composure. "It feels like you're turning the system against me," he said, his voice wavering. "You're exploiting the laws that favour you, pushing me aside as if I don't matter. Why are you being so heartless?"

Yetunde's expression hardened, her face flushing with anger. Her defences went up in an instant, a cold fury replacing the indifference. "You don't have the authority to determine what is in my best interest. You've made this situation unbearable, and I have every right to make decisions that protect me and my children." Don't try to manipulate me into feeling guilty for that."

Afolabi remained composed, even as a whirlwind of emotions raged within him. "I've tried everything to save our marriage. I've respected your wishes, given you the space you requested, and done all I could to provide for our family. And this is how you repay me?"

"I have no interest in your rhetoric or in engaging in a debate," Yetunde snapped. "I've made up my mind. If you wish to engage in a debate, kindly find another venue for such discussions. I'm resolute in my decision and won't be swayed."

As Yetunde turned away, leaving Afolabi alone with his heartbreak, the weight of his predicament crashed over him like an overwhelming force. He had a limited amount of time to figure out his life. As he confronted the prospect of returning to Nigeria, a place he had longed to escape, the hope of a new beginning felt like a distant dream.

The following day, the situation took a turn for the worse. Afolabi arrived at work, ready to immerse himself in his responsibilities and escape into his tasks. However, as he sat down to log in to the system, his manager's serious expression hinted at more troubling developments. "Afolabi," the manager began, "we received a letter from the Home Office this morning. Your work permit has been revoked with immediate effect."

Afolabi's breath hitched in his throat as he absorbed the news. "What am I supposed to do now?" he murmured; his voice barely audible.

"I apologise, Afolabi," his manager said, with a hint of compassion in his tone. "There seems to be no solution available. I'm sorry, but you'll need to vacate the premises immediately."

Afolabi felt as though the ground was shifting beneath him. The loss of his work permits only deepened the weight of his already overwhelming situation. He packed all his things, dropped his laptop, and quietly left the office. As he walked down the street, he was consumed by a sense of confusion, each step heavy with the gravity of what lay ahead.

Two days later, Afolabi sat in the dimly lit living room, his mind tangled in a storm of doubt and confusion. The weight of recent events pressed upon him, and a palpable tension filled the air, thick and stifling.

The silence was shattered when Yetunde entered, her steps measured and resolute. She faced him, her expression cold and unfaltering.

"I can't stand having you here any longer, Afolabi," she said, her voice icy and resolute. "You need to leave this house, and you need to do it now." Her words landed with the weight of finality, closing off any chance of reprieve.

Afolabi glanced up at her, his heart racing in his chest. "What are you talking about, Yetunde? Where is this coming from?"

Her gaze sharpened, and she folded her arms, leaning in slightly to emphasise her words. "I need my freedom, but if you refuse to leave, I will call the police for you and tell them you are molesting me." "You're familiar with how things operate here. They'll believe me instead of you, and you'll be gone in the blink of an eye." Afolabi's face turned pale as the colour drained from it. He gazed at her, a mixture of astonishment and growing unease evident on his face. "Yetunde, are you really serious?" That statement isn't correct. How could one possibly consider the notion of engaging in such an evil and callous act?

"Don't push me, Afolabi," she whispered, her voice dripping with venom. "I've reached my limit. I've had enough of you and want you to leave now."

The room felt suffocating as Afolabi grappled with understanding her words. The woman he had once loved, the mother of his children, now posed a grave threat to everything he held dear. He understood the potential consequences of her unfounded accusations, recognising they had the power to destroy his reputation in the eyes of the law.

Feeling the weight of impending loss, Afolabi urgently grabbed his phone and dialled Bayo's number. "Bayo," Afolabi began, his voice filled with intense emotion. "I... I'm not sure where to start. The world is crumbling. It seems like everything is going wrong for me. I've lost my work permit and have just been evicted by my wife. She's threatening to involve the police if I don't leave immediately, Bayo. I'm feeling quite frightened... I'm at a loss for what to do." Bayo's voice came through the phone, exuding calmness while also expressing genuine concern.

"Afolabi, I'm really sorry to hear that. Listen, take a deep breath and try to stay calm. I can tell that staying there isn't an option, but we'll definitely find a solution. Why don't you come by my place for now? We can figure things out from there."

Afolabi silently acknowledged Bayo's words, his emotions a complex blend of appreciation and hopelessness. "Thank you, Bayo," he replied softly. "I don't know what I'd do without you. I'll be there soon."

Bayo offered words of reassurance, promising they would tackle the challenges together, step by step. "You've got someone by your side, my brother. Just take it easy, and we'll figure this out."

After hanging up, Afolabi took a deep breath, sensing a glimmer of hope in the midst of the darkness Despite the fear, betrayal, and uncertainty that weighed on him, there was comfort in knowing he had someone he could trust. With Bayo's support and his own determination, Afolabi resolved to face whatever lay ahead. It was going to be a difficult road, but he remained hopeful that a solution existed—one that would help him escape this nightmare and secure his future.

The weight of Yetunde's choices and the chain of unfortunate events left him uncertain about what lay ahead. His mind wandered to Dara and Dami, and a strong urge to protect them from the consequences compelled him to explore all available sources of assistance.

Bayo's humble flat stood in stark contrast to the grandeur of the home Afolabi had been forced to abandon. The small living room, adorned with minimalistic decor, offered a brief escape from the tumultuous events that had engulfed Afolabi's life. As he reclined on the worn-out couch, trying to decipher his fragmented reality, he found himself grappling with the burden of betrayal and injustice.

The initial evening at Bayo's house was filled with restless contemplation. The couch was less than ideal, and the never-ending noise of cars on the busy Hoe Street in Walthamstow only added salt to injury.

As the sun rose the next day, Bayo stepped out of his bedroom and offered Afolabi a warm cup of tea. They sat at the small kitchen table; their silence laden with unspoken thoughts worries.

As Bayo spoke, Afolabi felt a complex mix of gratitude and vulnerability. The tension within his family was palpable as they struggled with the reality that Yetunde held the power to determine his future-a bitter truth he found hard to accept. The weight of his family's anxieties only deepened his own sense of helplessness.

Afolabi could not help but feel the overwhelming burden of his circumstances, which seemed unfair and almost unbearable. Bayo, recognising his unease, extended a reassuring gesture by placing his hand on the man's shoulder.

"Keep pushing, don't give up, Afolabi. We'll make it through this. I'm fully committed to assisting you, and together, we will find a solution."

Despite Bayo's reassuring words, Afolabi's future remained shrouded in uncertainty. His once steady life had crumbled into a series of legal conflicts and emotional struggles. As he reclined on Bayo's couch, his eyes fixed on the ceiling, a spark of hope flickered within him. Despite the overwhelming odds, he longed for a chance to rebuild his life and embrace his children once more.

Chapter 12

Reflection and Resolve

In the aftermath of the tragedy, Afolabi was overwhelmed by a deep sense of hopelessness. The weight of Yetunde's betrayal, coupled with the uncertainty of his future in the UK, hung over him like a dark, suffocating cloud. Each morning, he woke to the harsh reality of his new life-one stripped of the comfort and security that his loved ones had once provided. Nevertheless, even during the most challenging moments, Afolabi was determined to find a path forward. His deep affection for his daughters, Dara and Dami, served as a guiding light, leading him through the difficult times of his anguish.

The sparsely furnished room he now called home consisted of only a bed, a table, and a chair. Each night, as he lay awake on the couch, the walls, painted a monotonous shade of grey, seemed to gradually constrict around him, creating a suffocating atmosphere. The once vibrant echoes of his daughters' joyous giggles and the reassuring company of Yetunde were now engulfed in an oppressive silence.

One evening, after yet another disappointing day of seeking guidance and trying to make sense of his broken life, Afolabi found himself sitting on the edge of the sofa, his hands clasped together in prayer. The softness of his voice barely concealed the intensity of his words, which overflowed with unfiltered emotion. "Oh, I'm at a loss for what to do. I'm overwhelmed with confusion and disappointment. Lord God, please provide me with guidance and assist me in finding a solution to remain in the UK for the sake of my beloved daughters."

As he concluded his prayer, Afolabi felt an unusual serenity enveloping him. It was as if, at that moment, he had relinquished his troubles to a greater force, trusting that, somehow, everything would fall into place. He rose from his seat, approached the modest window, and gazed out at the bustling city below. The streetlights flickered in the distance, and a glimmer of hope washed over him, breaking through the darkness that had consumed him for days.

The following day, Afolabi decided to connect with the Nigerian community in Walthamstow. He had learned about the local group that provided assistance to immigrants facing challenges, and he understood that reaching out to individuals who had experienced something similar could give him the resilience and direction he needed.

At the community centre, Afolabi felt a mix of optimism and anxiety. He approached a tall, broad-shouldered man who seemed to be in charge, greeting him with a friendly smile and self-assurance demeanour.

"Good afternoon," Afolabi greeted him, extending his hand. "My name is Afolabi, and I was informed that this community group might have the resources to assist me."

The man returned the greeting with a firm handshake, his eyes conveying a profound sense of empathy. "Good afternoon, Afolabi. My name is Chuka, and I am the coordinator of this centre. We're here to provide mutual support, particularly during difficult times. What issues are you currently facing?"

Afolabi paused briefly, uncertain about how much to disclose. However, Chuka's demeanour gave him the confidence to express himself freely. "I find myself in a rather challenging predicament," Afolabi began. "My wife... Her actions have placed me in a precarious position, jeopardising my immigration status. I'm at a loss about where to begin to remain in the UK for the sake of my daughters.

Chuka nodded solemnly, his ruddy round face exhibiting a serious demeanour. "I understand, brother. We have all faced similar obstacles. The immigration system can be harsh and unyielding, especially when family dynamics come into play. But don't be discouraged. There are ways around this, and we will do everything we can to assist you."

They spent the next hour exploring Afolabi's situation, with Chuka offering practical guidance and a comforting presence. By the end of the conversation, Afolabi felt a renewed inspiration. He had a support system that helped him through his struggles, and witnessing others triumph over similar obstacles fueled his determination to persevere.

That evening, as Afolabi made his way back to Bayo's modest home, a strong sense of resolve settled in his heart. The sting of Yetunde's betrayal still haunted him, but it no longer held him captive. He had made the decision to remain in the UK, support his daughters, and begin anew, regardless of the challenges that lay ahead.

Chapter 13

The Weight of Regret

As Afolabi gradually found his way and adjusted to the reality of life, Yetunde grappled with a different type of chaos. The freedom and independence she had initially sought with pride suddenly turned sour. The stillness within the house, once a sanctuary of solace, now weighed heavily on her spirit. She strolled through the rooms that once resounded with the joyful laughter of her loved ones, feeling a pang of sorrow grip her heart. The twins became less active, refused food, and cried more often, calling for their father even in their sleep. After a while, they fell ill, which Yetunde, though a qualified nurse, found quite troublesome. All the tests conducted on them came back negative. Finally, it was discovered that the girls were experiencing paediatric depression as a result of their father's absence.

One evening, as Yetunde prepared the children's favourite dinner-beans and fried plantain, hoping to lift their spirits, she caught a glimpse of herself in the kitchen window. The woman staring back seemed unfamiliar. Her eyes were heavy with exhaustion, her posture slumped, and her face wore a hollow emptiness, a stark contrast to the confident woman she had once been. She had once prided herself on being in control, but now that sense of command felt like a distant mirage, its promise accompanied by unforeseen consequences.

"Dara and Dami," she called softly, her voice laced with hope. "Guess what? Mummy made your favourite meal. Come and enjoy it."

"What about Daddy? Is he eating with us as well?"

Yetunde was at a loss for what to say. What excuse could she give for their father's absence?

"Be good, my precious babies," she said softly, trying to reassure them. "Mummy will carry you to the table and feed you. I know you'll like it."

"I want my Daddy!" the two girls cried, all at once, their tears flowing uncontrollably. This was overwhelming for Yetunde, who was already stretched thin by the demands of her job and the task of managing the twins. She had made countless, fruitless attempts to find a live-in childminder, but to no avail. She was on the brink of tears as she watched them look with disgust at the food she had so diligently prepared. They slid down from their chairs, went into the bedroom, occupied the side of the bed where their father used to sleep, and hugged his pillow. Soon, the girls fell asleep and began mumbling.

It was heart-wrenching for Yetunde, who watched helplessly as her daughters pined away. She seemed to lose her appetite for food as well. In that moment, Dami suddenly stirred, smiling in her sleep as she said, "Daddy, tell us a story." Then, she woke up abruptly and looked around. When she saw her mother instead of her father, her face crumpled, and she let out a wail so sharp and heartbreaking that Dara, still asleep, was startled awake and joined in the wailing cries. The sound of their grief echoed through the house, and Yetunde, feeling helpless, could only watch as her daughters' pain deepened.

"A story? Don't worry, Mummy will tell you a story. Okay?" she said in a soft, teary voice. She began the familiar tale of the princess and the frog.

But halfway through, Dara interrupted, "I don't like this story."

"Me too," Dami chimed in. "We want the one Daddy tells us."

She cuddled them affectionately to herself and stared blankly ahead in confusion. She could no longer stop her tears and let them flow freely. This seemed to have a magical effect on the twins, who, after a while, fell asleep.

After settling the girls into bed, Yetunde sat alone in the living room, the weight of her decisions pressing heavily on her. She recalled her conversations with Lola, her dearest friend— words of both encouragement and concern, each pulling her in different directions.

"Yetunde," Lola had said, her voice slightly above a whisper during one of their coffee outings, a deliberate attempt to underscore the gravity of what she was about to share and ensure the

conversation remained private. "There's this saying: *regret has no medicine*. In other words, *'had I known'* always comes too late. For me, it's like the soundtrack to the consequences of poor

choices."

Lola went on to recount the story of a young woman who had been profoundly troubled by her husband's misconduct. Determined to leave him, she insisted on a divorce, despite pleas from friends and family to reconsider. She refused to listen. Over time, she adopted an air of defiance, becoming an empress of her own making, unwilling to take orders from anyone. She obtained the divorce and secured custody of the children, but it did not bring her peace. She still wanted more—she wished for him to lose his job as well.

But the court had ruled that he would be responsible for the children's upkeep and education. Then, an opportunity arose for the man to travel overseas. He left quietly, cutting off all contact with her. It was only then that she awoke to the painful reality: neither the court nor her family or friends could alter what she had brought upon herself.

"I understand your desire to establish independence, especially in a foreign land where everything seems daunting. However, it is important not to lose sight of what truly matters. "Afolabi is your husband; he has been kind, valuing and cherishing you. It's only fair that you treat him with the same respect."

At the time, Yetunde had dismissed Lola's concerns, confident in her own judgment regarding what was best for her and her children. But now, sitting alone in the dimly lit room, Lola's words echoed in her mind, stirring a quiet sense of unease.

Even Olakunle, the one responsible for the collapse of her marriage, dared not speak to her again.

Yetunde visited Olakunle's house one evening. When she arrived, she realised she couldn't open the door—it was locked from the inside. Knocking and banging on the door in frustration, Olakunle finally emerged, his face twisted with frustration anger.

"Who are you and what do you want? Who are you looking for?" he had asked gruffly in a row. His eyes were red with anger, and his face bore the semblance of a ferocious beast ready to pounce on its prey. "Now, listen, and listen very well. If you know what's good for your life, don't ever come anywhere near me again. Got it? You bitch!" After unleashing a torrent of obscenities, he turned around and lifted the new woman up, kissing her as he entered the room, which left Yetunde in shock. From that day she caught him with another woman when she visited unannounced, she realised that in her pursuit of securing her future, she had unintentionally distanced herself from the one who had never raised his voice against her, let alone abused her, and who had supported her through every high and low. As shame washed over her, she left Olakunle's house dejected, her heart heavy with regret.

It was then that the truth truly dawned on

her: Olakunle had been playing with her emotions and vulnerabilities all along, using her fears and insecurities as his own game.

As the night dragged on, Yetunde found herself unable to find any rest. Restless and agitated, her thoughts consumed her as she struggled to find peace. At last, overwhelmed by the burden of her guilt, she mustered the courage to pick up her phone and call her mother. After a few beeps, the phone line was connected.

"Hello, omo mi."

"Maami, I'm sorry for disturbing you this late." Yetunde apologised on hearing her mother's sleepy voice.

"No problem. How are my granddaughters and your husband?"

At the mention of Olakunle, Yetunde's composure cracked. She broke down completely, sobbing with anguish.

"Kilo nshele? What happened?" her mother asked, her voice filled with confusion.

"It's all ruined... ruined... I ruined it all," Yetunde choked out between sobs.

"Talk slowly; I want to understand. How do you mean?"

"Maami, please forgive me for being a disobedient daughter."

"You're still not saying anything. Besides, you didn't offend me. So why asking for forgiveness?"

"I … I… I drove him out of the house." Yetunde's voice faltered, her chest heaving with each desperate breath. The chair creaked under her, echoing the weight of her sorrow.

"You're getting me more confused," the poor woman said honestly, struggling to understand this kind of situation. "You drove who?"

"I did, Maami." She answered like a little child caught in wrongdoing. "I sent Afolabi out of the house".

"And why?" she asked in a panic, feeling a bitter taste in her mouth. "Please, give me a few minutes; I want to use the toilet." She was drenched in sweat, dropped the phone without hanging up, and rushed off. When she returned and picked up the phone, Yetunde opened up and told her everything. "Maami, my life has been miserable since I took that action. The children can't stop crying because they want their father back. I want to go back to him, but how can I face him?" Yetunde sighed helplessly.

"Well, we can only put our trust in God." The mother replied after a long period of silence. She desperately fought back the tears that were forcing their way out of her eyes to maintain a composed tone and figure out a solution. "Is there anyone you know whom your husband respects greatly?"

"Yes, Maami. His elder sister and pastor," Adewale."

"Alright then, speak to them. I'll make my own little effort. I'll discuss it with your father in the morning."

"But Maami, I can't face Sister Bolanle. I was very rude to her. I really don't know what came over me."

"Speak to the Pastor first," her mother urged gently.

"Thank you, Maami," Yetunde whispered, her voice filled with gratitude before hanging up.

Yetunde's mother did exactly as she promised. She visited Afolabi's parents in Lagos, taking all the local food items she knew were not readily available but highly prized by people in the city and presented them to them humbly.

Afolabi's mother was dumbfounded when she saw the two big sacks. "How were you able to carry this heavy load all the way from Ijero Ekiti to Lagos?"

"It's nothing," Yetunde's mother replied with a small, weary smile.

After exchanging some pleasantries, Yetunde's mother cleared her throat and got straight to the point. "My in-law, first, I want to thank you from the depths of my heart for welcoming me into your home. Given the current circumstances, not many would. You have every reason not to allow me into your abode." She choked back her emotions and lowered her head. When she raised her head again, her eyes were red with sorrow. "I'm only here to understand your perspective. I am so ashamed of my daughter's actions."

Afolabi's mother was moved by the raw sincerity in her voice. "My in-law, you don't need to chastise yourself like this."

"How can I not?" Yetunde's mother replied, her voice shaking. "This girl wasn't like this when she was with us. At least you can testify to that. Now anyone who hears it must certainly point at me as a mother who did not give her daughter a proper upbringing. I feel so sad that your son bore all this alone and never complained to us. Now that she has come to her senses and told me the truth, I'm here to sincerely apologise to you and Afolabi, even though he's not here. Second, I want to offer my unreserved apology to Bolanle; it is only a fool who bites the hand that feeds him. I wouldn't mind kneeling before her had she been here, regardless of the age difference." She stood up abruptly and knelt before Afolabi's mother, tears streaming down her face. "What face do I still have before you? Finally, I want to say we're truly sorry for all the pain we caused Afolabi and your entire family."

Afolabi's mother was moved to tears; she hugged her and helped her up. The two of them cried for a while and then comforted each other. They had a brief discussion, and Yetunde's mother stood up to go.

"I'll call Bolanle, my daughter, and explain things to her." Afolabi's mother promised. They bade each other farewell as Yetunde's mother took her leave.

Bolanle did not want to have anything to do with Yetunde ever again. The pain of her callous behaviour towards Afolabi and the way she had humiliated her over the phone was still fresh in her memory.

"Mum is talking about reconciliation," Bolanle fumed. "Reconciliation with who? To give her the opportunity to kill my only brother? Never!" These were her thoughts as she spoke with her mother. "Mum, is Yetunde the only woman in this world?" "Certainly not.

But what guarantee do you have that others will be better? Don't forget that there are children in between. Have you thought it through? You don't throw away the bathwater with the child inside."

Mother and daughter argued back and forth until Bolanle unwillingly gave in to her mother out of respect.

Meanwhile, Yetunde took time off work and went to see Pastor Adewale in his office. She needed guidance, and he was the one person she felt could offer it. Pastor Adewale greeted her warmly, offering her a cup of hot tea to ward off the chilly weather.

"Wow! "It's wonderful to see you, Sister Yetunde!" he said with a sincere smile. "You've been away from the fellowship for quite some time. We've truly missed you."

"I'm sorry, Pastor," Yetunde replied, guilt weighing heavily on her heart. She sat down gracefully, accepting the tea, but the warmth of the cup did little to soothe her. She almost lost her appetite but forced herself to take a sip, hoping that the gesture would provide some comfort

Sensing her distress, Pastor Adewale shifted the conversation. "So, how's work going? How have you been managing?"

"Pastor, had it not been for my professional background, I would have broken down long ago," she admitted, her voice a mix of frustration and sadness

"It clearly shows on your face. You look emaciated. Do you actually get enough rest after your shifts?" he asked with a fatherly tone voice.

"Not at all, Pastor," Yetunde confessed, her voice faltering. "I'm under terrible self-induced pressure. My daughters are sick, and I feel powerless to do anything." Her voice broke, and the tears she had been holding back finally streamed down her face. She covered her face with her hands, her chest heaving violently, causing her winter jacket to jerk with each sob.

Pastor Adewale waited patiently, giving her the space to grieve. After a few moments, he spoke, his voice kind yet firm. "Sister Yetunde, pull yourself together and listen to me."

Yetunde calmed herself down, even though her face was still swollen with tears. She took a piece of tissue and wiped her nostrils. She had never been the makeup type, so she couldn't care less about such trifles. She wiped her face clean with a brown handkerchief, looked up at Pastor Adewale, and listened intently.

He shifted slightly in his chair, glancing at the wall clock before continuing with a steady tone. "I'm neither a psychotherapist nor a professional counsellor, but I've learned a great deal from my years of experience and the help of God. I allowed you to cry for a while because I understand the various roles that tears play in life. Let me highlight just two."

He adjusted himself on the chair, looked at the wall clock opposite him and continued.

"First, tears serve as a purgative for emotional pain. However, they can become negative when excessive. The second function is outright negative, which I briefly mentioned in my previous statement. This type induces both physical and emotional suffering. It arises from frustration, bitterness, and desperation. Such tears amplify feelings of humiliation and rejection, which have driven some to attempt suicide in extreme cases. They become a tonic for vengeance and hatred. In fact, the list is endless. Two characters in the Bible exemplify this: the first is Esau, and the second is Saul, the king. Esau's tears had nothing to do with repentance; neither did the pain and hatred in his heart dissipate; instead, they fueled his resolve to kill his brother. The same is true of Saul, the king, who relentlessly pursued David to kill him. Now, the person behind the scenes is the enemy, the devil. But thanks be to God who shields us from him schemes."

"Amen!" Yetunde echoed, Wow! Pastor, this is an eye-opener for me."

"Sister Yetunde, now that you're feeling a bit better, let's address the reason for your visit."

"Pastor, I can't thank you enough for everything you've done for my family," Yetunde said humbly, her voice thick with emotion. "It's all my fault, and I want to make amends for my errors." She told Pastor Adewale everything from beginning to end. When she finished speaking, she sighed heavily, lowering her head in shame.

Pastor Adewale listened quietly, his calm demeanour never faltering. "Do you think this situation is hopeless?" Pastor Adewale asked calmly with a smile on his face.

Yetunde was at a loss for words. "Pastor, I really don't know." "Let's turn to the Bible," he suggested, reaching for one of the Bibles on his desk and handing it to her. "Open to Ecclesiastes 9:4. It says, 'For to him that is joined to all the living there is hope: for a living dog is better than a dead lion.' Does this answer your question?"

Yetunde looked at the verse, her heart racing with hope. "Yes, Pastor," she said, her voice full of new understanding. She read the verse again as if seeing it for the first time.

Well, we thank God for answering our prayers. Your breakup with Olakunle is a testimony to that. He was an agent of darkness sent to destroy your family and destiny. During your relationship, you turned against honest friends and family who could protect you.

"By the way, did you people hear from God before your decision to relocate, or were you simply carried away by the Japa syndrome?"

"We honestly did not hear anything; we were just driven by our own dreams, although we prayed." she responded truthfully.

"Well, that explains everything. You see, he succeeded because, first, your altar was broken. Second, your sex life was zero; when you feel like it, you don't ask because you believe he must always be the one to initiate. And so, the enemy took advantage of that gap to strike. You were actually under a spell, but thank God for His mighty power and deliverance.

Yetunde's eyes welled up with tears of relief as the weight of his words sank in. "Thank God, Pastor. I feel like I can finally breathe again."

I will call Brother Afolabi, your husband, to discuss this with him. When you get home, call him and inform him about his daughters not feeling fine."

Yetunde smiled faintly, a glimmer of hope finally returning to her eyes. "Thank you so much, Pastor. I will do exactly as you've said." Just as she was about to stand, Pastor Adewale's voice stopped her. "Let us pray. Lord Jesus, we thank you for always being there for us; through thick and thin, you're still by our side! What would we do without you? We give you glory, honour, and praise. Lord, you're the potter; we're the clay. We ask, therefore, Father, that you mend this broken marriage, heal everyone, and restore peace and joy to this family. In Jesus name, we pray, Amen."

That evening, Pastor Adewale called Afolabi and convinced him not to dismiss Yetunde's wish for communication, which gained his approval.

"Pastor, I will listen to you. However, my heart is filled with pain. The information I possess—not just hearsay but concrete evidence of her behaviour and wrongdoing towards me—is staggering. In the past, I installed tracking software that I designed on her mobile phone and also on mine for trial purposes. The tracker transmits all the data to cloud storage in real time and leaves no traces on its host. She forgot about the tracker I installed in her presence and continued with her escapades. I, too, forgot about the tracker until my eviction. Determined to uncover the reasons for my troubles, I remembered the tracker and was horrified by the information I retrieved. How many men can stand it."

"Jesus went to the cross to purchase our pardon. Don't cling to the past. Instead, let's thank God for the answer to our prayer. Don't lose sight of what God revealed the day you came to see me in my office. Brother Afolabi." Pastor Adewale urged.

Afolabi sat in silence for a long moment, the weight of Pastor Adewale's words settling in. "Alright, Pastor," he finally said, his voice hoarse. "I'll listen to you. But you must understand… it's hard. Harder than anything I've ever faced."

That evening, Yetunde fell into deep thought. "Should I call or send a text message? What if he doesn't answer my call?" Eventually, she settled for the latter. She picked up her phone and sent Afolabi a text message: "Please, can we have a conversation? Your girls are sick and won't accept food anymore. I believe it is necessary for you to come round and see them. They're missing you terribly." The following day, they met in the living room, a place that had once brought them comfort but now seemed filled with tension. Dami and Dara clung to their father as if they hadn't seen him for years. Yetunde noticed the anguish on Afolabi's face, the visible signs of stress and fatigue that had previously been absent. She gasped deeply, her heart racing in her chest.

"Afolabi," she began, her voice quivering, "I've been contemplating quite a bit." I now realise that I have made a grave error—a truly dreadful one. I became so consumed with seeking superficial happiness that I lost sight of what truly holds significance. I'm so sorry. I deeply regret the pain I have caused you and our daughters."

Afolabi gazed at her, a storm of emotions brewing in his eyes. "Yetunde, you didn't just hurt me," he said, his voice low and pained. "You have deceived me. Everything we built together has been completely taken away. Can you even begin to grasp the impact it has had on me?"

The words struck her like a physical blow; her emotions overwhelmed her, and her eyes filled with tears as she fought to keep herself composed. She took a deep breath, forcing herself to stay calm.

"I do understand, Afolabi," she said softly, her voice trembling. "I see it every day in how you look at me, in the silence between us. It's as if you're a stranger, and I've made you that way. It fills me with such guilt that I can hardly breathe. I want to fix this, but... I don't even know how to go about it."

The room was thick with silence as Afolabi sat there, his gaze fixed on her, yet his mind was miles away. He did not speak for a long moment, the weight of his thoughts pressing down on him like an unbearable storm. His heart was in turmoil, caught between two opposing forces.

One part of him—small, fragile—still longed for her. He wanted to believe in the possibility of forgiveness, of starting fresh, of mending the broken pieces of their bond. He imagined, for a fleeting moment, that things could somehow be repaired, that trust could be rebuilt. But the other part of him, still raw with pain, could not ignore the truth of what he had uncovered. That part of him questioned whether he could ever trust her again. Could he really?

The betrayal cut deeper than any wound he had known, and the echoes of her lies seemed to vibrate in every corner of his mind. Could he ever forget what he now knew about her: the hidden places, the secrets, the unspoken truth? Would he ever look at her the same way again? Afolabi felt a sharp pang in his chest, the familiar ache of love mingled with the bitter sting of doubt. He wanted to believe in her, to believe that the woman he once knew, the woman he had loved, was still there beneath the surface. But the evidence, the tracker, the reality – it all painted a different picture, one he could not ignore.

His mind kept circling back to one singular thought: Can you trust someone who has already betrayed you once?

It was a question that made him uneasy, one he did not know how to answer. Could love overcome this betrayal? Could time heal what had been broken? Or was this the point of no return? Every part of him was torn, pulled between the man he still wanted to be—the one willing to forgive—and the man who had learned the hard way.

At last, he spoke, his voice heavy with exhaustion and weariness. "I'm not sure if we can resolve this, Yetunde. The trust we had... it has been entirely shattered."

Chapter 14

Seeking Redemption

Making the decision to mend their relationship was no simple task. Afolabi and Yetunde were well aware of the challenges that lay ahead of them—a path filled with difficult discussions and the need to address the underlying issues that had caused their separation. They chose to seek professional help through counselling, hoping to find a way to heal the deep wounds they had suffered endured.

Their initial counselling session was filled with tension. Afolabi and Yetunde sat at opposite ends of the small room, each displaying a sense of caution and doubt. The therapist, a calm and empathetic woman of Caribbean descent named Dr. Natasha, welcomed them with a friendly smile.

"Thank you both for coming today," she began, her tone warm. "This is a welcoming environment where you are encouraged to share your emotions freely and sincerely. Let's start by talking about what brought you here. I want you to be very honest and... sincere."

Yetunde glanced at Afolabi, trying to read his expression for any hint of his emotions. However, his face remained inscrutable as he stared intently at a particular spot on the floor. With a deep breath, she mustered the courage to take the lead. "I..." She confessed, her voice trembling, that she had made choices that had deeply hurt Afolabi. "It appears that my previous actions, which I thought were in the best interest of our family, were misguided. I allowed my own fears and stubbornness to dictate my actions, resulting in the loss of everything we held dear."

Dr Natasha nodded with an encouraging smile. "Admitting our mistakes requires a great deal of courage. But can you be more explicit?"

Yetunde hesitated for a moment before admitting, "I was caught off guard... I cheated on him."

"So, Afolabi, what are your thoughts on Yetunde's statement?"

Afolabi raised his head, locking eyes with the therapist before shifting his attention to Yetunde. His tone was composed, yet there was a subtle undertone of frustration, a hint of suppressed ire. "I can't help but feel a sense of betrayal. I sense a lack of trust from the woman I married, the mother of my children when it comes to making decisions together. She completely ignored my...presence."

Yetunde flinched at his words, feeling the guilt twisting inside her. "I understand, Afolabi. I deeply apologise for my actions. I had my doubts about you, and I must admit, I was mistaken. I understand that now. However, I am determined to resolve this. I want to regain that trust if you are willing to give me the chance."

Dr Natasha stepped in, her voice calm and reassuring. "Trust is a delicate issue; once it shatters, it requires dedication and patience to mend. However, achieving success is within reach if both parties are committed to putting in the effort. Afolabi, are you willing to consider opening yourself up to that possibility?"

Afolabi fell into a brief silence, his eyes fixed on Yetunde. He could sense the depth of emotion in her gaze, the urgency to rectify the situation. However, the pain lingered, weighing him down with an uncertain ability to overcome it. "I don't know," he finally admitted. "I'm willing to give it a try for the sake of our daughters, but it will require some effort and time."

The therapy sessions continued over the following weeks, each unraveling a deeper layer of pain and frustration that had long been concealed. They discussed their fears, disappointments, and the ways they had let each other down. It was a gradual and sometimes challenging journey, but as they continued their sessions, they began to uncover the deep-seated pain and lack of trust, ultimately revealing the enduring love that had remained hidden. First, Afolabi had to agree to move back to their home after a series of persuasive efforts by Pastor Adewale, Bayo, and their parents back home Nigeria.

They began making subtle alterations to their home. They cherished quality family time, taking Dara and Dami to the park together or engaging in fun games in the living room. They started dividing the household chores, silently recognising their shared commitment.

One evening, after the girls had been put to bed, Yetunde saw Afolabi sitting at the kitchen table, gazing through the window. She approached him cautiously, uncertain of his desire for solitude. "May I accompany you?" she inquired gently.

Afolabi gave a slight nod, and she took a seat across from him. They sat in silence for a while, the only sound being the rhythmic ticking of the clock on the wall.

Finally, Yetunde spoke, her voice barely above a whisper. "I miss us, Afolabi. I miss the way things used to be."

Afolabi looked at her, his demeanour becoming gentler. "I miss us too, Yetunde. However, we have undergone significant changes since those events. We've evolved."

"I understand," she replied, her eyes filling with tears. "But maybe... maybe that's not such a bad thing. Perhaps we have the chance to be better, to become something stronger than we were before."

Afolabi reached across the table and gently took her hand, his touch warm and reassuring. "Maybe we can," he said, a faint smile tugging at the corner of his mouth lips.

The following day, Afolabi had just brought the children back from school and was in the living room, his hands resting on his knees as he watched the children run up and down the living room. The shock of being let go from his job still hadn't worn off. He had spent the last few weeks trying to figure out how to navigate this mess. His phone buzzed the screen lighting up with an unfamiliar number. He hesitated for a moment before answering.

"Hello?" he said, his voice tinged with uncertainty.

"Afolabi? It's Rachael from BT Human Resources. How have you been?"

Afolabi froze, his breath escaping him for a moment. He hadn't expected to hear from her, not after everything that had occurred. The call felt almost surreal.

"Hi, Rachael... I—uh, I wasn't expecting your call," Afolabi stammered. "How are you?"

"I'm doing well, thanks for asking," Rachael replied, her tone warm and familiar. "Listen, I know this is a bit out of the blue, but I've been following up on your situation, and I have some good news for you." you."

Afolabi straightened, his pulse quickening. "Good news?"

"Yes," Rachael continued, "I've been discussing the report we received from your manager with the management, particularly regarding the vacuum your absence has created. I am pleased to inform you that we have reviewed your case, and the company has agreed to provide you with a Certificate of Sponsorship."

Afolabi's heart skipped a beat. He had not anticipated anything like this, and the unexpected weight of the offer caught him completely off guard. "But… why? Why are you doing this? I thought—"

"I'm aware of your situation," Rachael interrupted gently. "When you left, we all knew you were going through a tough time. But you've always been a valuable contributor to the team, Afolabi. We don't want to lose you over something like this. We want you back if you're willing."

The words hung between them, suspended in the air. Afolabi felt a tightness in his chest, as if the burden of his failure, his pain, and now this unexpected chance was all weighing down on him at once. Although an appointment with Barrister Oludare had already been scheduled to discuss reinstating his dependant visa, he found himself silent for a moment, overwhelmed by the magnitude of what had just occurred.

"That… that's a lot to take in," Afolabi finally said. "Rachael, I'm truly grateful, and I wholeheartedly accept the offer," he declared.

"We will start the process immediately and get back to you," Rachael said in an assuring manner.

He ended the call and sat in silence for what felt like an eternity, letting the words sink in. It was hard to believe, but there it was-a chance to rebuild, to move forward, to stand on his own without being a dependant on anyone's visa.

As time passed, the weight that had burdened their existence gradually lifted. The therapy sessions continued, and they were no longer consumed by anger and bitterness. Instead, their attention turned towards repairing the strained bond, rekindling the affection that had united them initially. One day, as they sat in the therapist's office, Dr. Natasha beamed at them, a sense of accomplishment shining in her eyes. "You've both made tremendous progress," she said with genuine warmth. "The progress you've made is a true reflection of your dedication to one another and your loved ones. "I'm sure that with ongoing commitment, you will keep developing and becoming more powerful as a team."

After the session, as they walked to the bus stop, Afolabi felt a newfound buoyancy in his stride, a sensation that had been absent for quite some time. He glanced over at Yetunde, who wore a gentle smile, and felt a rush of fondness toward her. Both of them had endured countless trials and tribulations, yet they remained determined to protect their loved ones.

That evening, they decided to do something special for Dara and Dami. They enjoyed a delightful meal at a charming Nigerian restaurant on Old Kent Road, famous for its mouth-watering jollof rice and fried plantains. As they gathered around the table, the girls animatedly discussed their day at school. Afolabi couldn't help but feel a profound sense of satisfaction. He had longed for the chance to create new memories with his loved ones and build a shared experience future.

After dinner, they took a bus home. As they strolled through the park, the girls bounding ahead, their giggles filling the twilight. Afolabi and Yetunde walked side by side, their hands occasionally touching as they strolled.

After a while, Yetunde spoke up, interrupting the peaceful silence that surrounded them. "Perhaps we should consider making this our permanent residence. I understand that our current situation may not align with our initial intentions. Still, our daughters are content here, and we have begun to establish a meaningful life for our family.

Afolabi nodded, deep in thought. "I've been pondering the same idea. This place... it feels like home to me. After all the trials we've faced, it's only fair that we explore the path ahead for ourselves and our daughters."

Yetunde beamed, a wave of relief washing over her. "I'm glad you feel that way, Afolabi. I envision a collaborative effort to create something truly remarkable."

As they strolled along, the sun started to descend, enveloping the park in a warm, radiant light. Afolabi gazed at Yetunde, her face bathed in a gentle glow, and a wave of optimism washed over him. They had experienced the depths of despair and triumphed over adversity, leaving behind indelible marks from their past. However, they had also discovered a path towards progress and continued their journey together.

Chapter 15

A Glimmer of Hope

Afolabi and Yetunde's decision to remain in the UK marked a pivotal moment in their lives. They had made a solemn promise to one another, their children, and the new life they were building together. With a renewed sense of purpose, they eagerly began mapping out their future—dreaming of a larger home, cultivating new friendships, and wholeheartedly supporting each other's professional endeavors.

Yetunde threw herself into her work, fueled by a newfound passion and increasing confidence. She undertook a one-year top-up course and received her pin as a mental health nurse from the National Medical Council (NMC).

One afternoon, as she was leaving the hospital, she received a call from Afolabi. The excitement in his voice was palpable as he shared the news of his recent promotion at work. "They've asked me to lead a new project," he explained, his voice brimming with pride. "It's a significant undertaking, but I believe I am ready for the challenge."

Yetunde beamed with pride, her heart overflowing with joy. "I'm incredibly proud of you, Afolabi. You are more than capable. Let's celebrate tonight!"

That evening, they gathered at the dinner table, raising their glasses to Afolabi's achievements and the promising future that lay ahead. Dara and Dami, unaware of the true significance of the moment, joyfully applauded, their genuine delight serving as a poignant reminder of the immense struggle Afolabi and Yetunde faced to maintain their family's unity.

As time passed, Afolabi and Yetunde's bond deepened, strengthened by the challenges they had overcome together. They recognized the value of effective communication, cultivated patience, and found joy in life's simple moments.

One weekend, with little more than a fleeting thought, they embarked on an unexpected journey to Harts Holiday Park, tucked away in the serene Kent countryside. The burden of London life—its unyielding pace and constant clamor—had begun to take its toll, and they yearned for the simplicity of nature, the gentle rhythm of a slower existence, if only for a while.

They found a cosy cottage by a serene lake in Sheerness, where the stillness of the water mirrored the peace they longed for. The cottage was nestled beneath rolling hills, its windows framed by the vibrant hues of autumn leaves, as though nature herself had painted the perfect backdrop for their escape. It was a refuge, a place where they could let go of the world and be together, free from any interruption. In that peaceful haven, time seemed to slow, and the bonds of family deepened with each shared moment.

At dawn, Afolabi stirred from his sleep, drawn by an unplanned urge to take a quiet walk by the tranquil lake. The morning air was crisp and invigorating, and the sky stretched above him in a brilliant shade of blue. As he wandered along the water's edge, his thoughts drifted to the long journey he and his love had shared. There had been moments of doubt—times when he questioned whether their love could survive the trials they faced. But now, standing in the soft glow of the rising sun, a quiet certainty settled over him. His heart, once torn between hope and fear, now seemed to rest in a place of clarity.

It was then that he spotted a rose blooming elegantly near the shore. Intrigued, he bent down to pluck it, drawn to its beauty. However, as his fingers brushed against the delicate petals, the sharp thorns pricked his skin. The pain was swift and piercing. Afolabi winced as blood from his hand stained the rose's stem. In that moment, he grasped a deeper truth: Glory, like the rose, is not without its thorns. The beauty he sought was inseparable from the cost it demanded. The thorns were part of the rose, just as the trials had become part of their journey in love. This realisation, though painful, was vital—it spoke to the essence of their journey and would resonate throughout the choices they made ahead.

Upon his return to the cottage, he found Yetunde peacefully seated on the porch, the gentle morning light enveloping her in a warm glow. Cradling a steaming cup of tea, she appeared lost in the stillness of the moment. As he approached, she looked up, and a smile bloomed on her face, her eyes lighting up with an affection that seemed to deepen with each passing day. The sight of her, serene and steadfast, filled his chest with a quiet warmth as if all the uncertainties of the world could melt away in her presence.

"Good morning, my Crown", she whispered, her voice like a soft breeze. "You're back early." She tilted her head slightly, her smile softening as she noticed the rose in his hand.

He held it out to her, its petals glistening in the sunlight. "I thought of you," he said, offering the bloom with a tenderness that mirrored the depth of his feelings for her.

Yetunde's heart fluttered as she reached out to take the rose, her fingers brushing against its smooth petals. At that moment, she felt a wave of affection for Afolabi—for the thoughtful gesture and the bond they had nurtured. However, as she grasped the stem, her hand was pricked by the thorns. She flinched, a sharp sting racing through her palm, but she held on tightly.

Her mind raced, momentarily distracted by the pain. So much like us, she thought, staring at the blood now beginning to drip from the tip of her finger. Beautiful, fragile, and yet... sharp. The rose, so delicate and perfect, had drawn blood from her just as their love had sometimes drawn from her own heart. The thorns, though unseen at the beginning, had always been there, part of the beauty they shared.

She looked up at Afolabi, his expression a mix of concern and hope. His forehead creased as he saw the blood, his hand instinctively reaching for hers, but she stopped him with a gentle shake of her head.

The pain was sharp yet fleeting—a small sacrifice for something so exquisite.

A small, bittersweet laugh escaped her lips. "I should have known," she whispered. "Even the most beautiful things come with their price."

Afolabi's gaze softened, and he carefully took her injured hand in his, his fingers brushing over the pinhole-like marks as if trying to soothe them. Yetunde watched him, her heart torn between love and the quiet acknowledgement of the inevitable struggles ahead. The thorns were part of the rose, and the rose was part of their love, just as the pain was part of their journey.

As she stared at the rose in her hand, she couldn't help but think of the days ahead, the challenges that lay in wait beyond the horizon. Would they be able to protect the delicate beauty of what they had built? Would the thorns—those unforeseen pains—begin to grow sharper, harder to bear? Yet, as she looked into Afolabi's eyes, her doubts started to quiet, replaced by the unspoken promise between them: they would face whatever challenges arose together.

"It's beautiful," she said softly, her voice steady now, as she placed the rose carefully in a vase beside her on the table. "But like us, it's not without its cost. And yet, it's worth it, don't you think?"

Afolabi nodded, his hand still holding hers. The warmth of his touch silently affirms their shared understanding. "Yes, it's worth it."

She rested her head against his shoulder, letting out a peaceful sigh. "And I will continue to fight for us, Afolabi. Regardless of the challenges that lie ahead, we shall confront them as a united front."

Chapter 16

A Legacy of Resilience and Hope

Over time, the bond between Afolabi and Yetunde only grew stronger, nourished by the moments they had experienced together and the obstacles they had overcome. They understood that their relationship would never reach perfection, as there would always be challenges to face and hardships to endure. However, they were acutely aware of their resilience and determination to confront life's trials.

One evening, as they sat together in the living room, watching their daughters play on the floor, Afolabi turned to Yetunde with a thoughtful expression. "Yetunde," he began softly, "I've been reflecting on our journey and all we've encountered along the way. There were moments of doubt, but we persevered and emerged victorious. And now, I want to ensure that we continue to advance, to strengthen our connection."

Yetunde gazed at him, her heart filled with overwhelming emotion. She understood his intention perfectly. Their bond had been put to the ultimate test, pushing them beyond their wildest expectations. Yet, they emerged from the ordeal with unbreakable strength and resilience. "What ideas are you considering?" she enquired, her voice brimming with curiosity.

Afolabi grinned, extending his hand towards her. "It crossed my mind that perhaps it's time we reaffirm our commitment to one another—just the two of us, in a location that holds sentimental value—a way to strengthen our bond and dedication to each other and to our loved ones."

Yetunde's eyes widened in surprise, and then a beaming smile illuminated her face. "Wow, Afolabi, that's a truly remarkable idea. That sounds great. It would serve as a poignant reflection of our journey and a joyous tribute to our enduring love."

They dedicated the following weeks to meticulously organising a cosy, personal ceremony. They chose to have it at the same lake where they had embarked on their inaugural family excursion after their reconciliation. It was a place that embodied fresh starts, tranquillity, and the resilience they had discovered in one another.

On the day of the event, the weather could not have been more perfect. The skies were clear, the sunlight warmed the surroundings, and a gentle breeze played with the leaves of the trees. Dara and Dami, adorned in identical white dresses, looked ethereal as they frolicked near the shoreline, their joyful giggles resonating throughout the tranquil lake.

Afolabi and Yetunde stood by the shore, their hands intertwined, as they planned to exchange vows once more in the presence of Pastor Adewale and a handful of the congregation. Their words were brimming with emotion, every promise laden with the depth of their shared past and the anticipation of what lay ahead.

"Afolabi," Yetunde began, her voice filled with raw emotion, "when we first got married, I realised that my love for you was just the beginning. I had yet to comprehend the true essence of creating a shared existence." Over the years, we have faced unexpected challenges, and I have made regrettable mistakes that have caused you significant pain. Yet, throughout it all, you have remained by my side, and I've come to understand the essence of genuine love. I promise to continue evolving with you, offering my unwavering support and treasuring each precious moment we share. I adore you now more than ever."

Afolabi then gently held her hand, his eyes glistening with tears. "Yetunde, when I married you, I sensed that we were embarking on an extraordinary adventure together. Little did I anticipate the countless challenges and obstacles that awaited us, putting our love to the ultimate test. Through all the challenges we have faced, our bond has grown stronger, and I am filled with gratitude, knowing you are always there for me. I solemnly vow to continue constructing our shared destiny, safeguarding our loved ones, and cherishing you wholeheartedly for eternity."

As they exchanged rings, their daughters joyfully ran over to join them, giggling and embracing their parents with love. They stood together, a tight-knit family, as the sun dipped below the horizon and the lake sparkled in the warm glow.

Later that evening, as they gathered around a cosy bonfire, toasting marshmallows and exchanging tales, the twins were eager to hear the story of the giant white wicked bird.

"OK, we'll continue from where we stopped, agreed?"

"Yes, Daddy!" they chorused. Even Yetunde, seeing their excitement, was curious; she recalled that gloomy evening when they had rejected both her food and her story.

One day, she came to pick vegetables from the garden, only to discover that someone had already been there before her

"Who has broken up Elephant's okra, Buffalo's *shokoyokoto* and Ram's Garden eggs?" she asked angrily, raising her voice.

"It's me. What can you do to me?" As these words fell, a giant white wicked bird descended on the poor old woman and beat her up mercilessly. After this, she dragged her broken body home and sat dejected in one corner of the house, waiting for the sons to come back home.

Soon after, the entire environment trembled with heavy footsteps. The poor old woman looked up expectantly, knowing this was a sure sign of her son's unmistakable approach, Elephant. When he entered the house, he noticed his mother's red eyes and immediately felt worried and impatient, with a raised trunk, a tapping foot, and a soft, rumbling trumpet. He asked, "Mother, what's wrong? What happened? Did anyone attack you?" His anger boiled over as he observed the marks of assault on her body

"Someone broke into your garden, ripped up all the vegetables, and beat me for daring to ask!" the poor old woman moaned.

"What? Who? My own mother…" he thundered in a rage, charging out of the house in a fit of fury, leaving a trail of destruction in his wake. "Come show me the culprit!" he trumpeted loudly, with a raised trunk and flapping ears. He walked so quickly that his mother could hardly keep up. However, things did not always go as expected. When they arrived, there was no one and nothing unusual to see. Both mother and son were surprised. After briefly scanning the surroundings, the elephant asked his mother to pose the same question that had first sparked the unprovoked attack. "Who has uprooted Elephant's okra, Buffalo's *shokoyokoto*, and Ram's Garden eggs?" she demanded confidently, following her son's prompting.

"It's me!" snapped the wicked white bird. "And what can you do to me?" He unleashed a series of irresistible attacks on mother and son at lightning speed, delivering such devastating blows that they left the Elephant dumbfounded and ashamed. Picking up his poor old mother from the ground, he dusted the sand off her body, laid her comfortably on his rough and wrinkled back, and walked slowly home with a lowered head and slumped shoulders, trumpeting mournfully along.

They were in this state when Buffalo returned. Upon learning what had happened, he could no longer contain his anger.

"Come and show me the fool, Mother!" he grunted, storming out of the house. The ground shook beneath his weight as he walked away. However, he met the same woeful defeat as those before him. So, they all sat forlorn in the house until Ram returned.

"Why is everyone mourning, Big Brothers?" he asked, deeply worried. But his big brothers, Elephant and Buffalo, were so embarrassed that they uttered not a word. They tactfully avoided his gaze. Thus, Ram turned to their mother, and upon seeing her swollen eyes, bruised face, open wounds on her skin, and ruffled hair, it was more than he could bear.

"Mother, who on earth did this to you?" he stammered in his voice of anger.

The mother was compelled to recount the entire story from start to finish, and he listened quietly without interruption.

"Mother, let's go and see that bird."

"What?" the mother asked alarm.

"Yes, let's go and see him," he replied confidently, taking the lead.

Reluctantly, the mother followed him, and he kept pace with her until they arrived at the location.

"Who has broken up Elephant's okra, Buffalo's *shokoyokoto*, and Ram's Garden eggs?"

Upon hearing this, the wicked giant white bird swooped down on them as it had before. However, Ram, who had remained vigilant throughout, powerfully and swiftly blocked all its ferocious attacks while simultaneously unleashing a barrage of deadly blows that left many of the bird's talons broken. The battle was so fierce that there was no room for retreat. As a result, the giant wicked white bird grew weaker, and its attacks became increasingly uncoordinated. In contrast, Ram's strength appeared undiminished; rather, it seemed to be growing, and his attacks were more focused and forceful than ever.

Then, the giant white wicked bird sent his friend Dog to fetch a supply of new claws for the fight. Ram also dispatched his friend, Mr. Goat, to bring him a supply of new horns. Along the way, the dog stumbled upon a clearing filled with all sorts of meat, both fresh and decayed. He promptly forgot his task, settled in one corner, and began to enjoy his good fortune. Meanwhile, Goat raced on without distraction, even though he spotted a basket of tempting yams. It was very alluring, but he deemed his errand more important. His friend required fresh horns to win the battle. Soon, he returned with a supply of new horns, which Ram quickly affixed. Then, with the new horns secured, Ram pushed forcefully against the enemy with even greater vigour than before.

The giant white wicked bird waited desperately in vain for a supply of new claws from his friend Dog, having already lost his remaining talons in the fight. At this point, Ram was stamping viciously down on his wings with his powerful hooves, preparing to deliver the final killing blow. Left with no option, the giant wicked white bird soared high into the sky and transformed into thunder. Simultaneously, Ram struck the ground with force, continuing his effort to defeat him in the fight.

"You see, that's why the ram always knocks the ground whenever it thunders, thinking the fight is still on." He smiled, looking into the daughters' eyes, which were full of excitement. Even Yetunde was spellbound by the story.

Afolabi could not help but feel a profound sense of satisfaction. After a gruelling and arduous journey, they had finally reached their destination. They had created a world brimming with affection, strength, and optimism. Leaning back on the couch, he folded his arms on his chest and closed his eyes.

A Fresh Start

With their vows renewed and their bond stronger than ever, Afolabi and Yetunde embarked on a new chapter of their lives filled with purpose and excitement. They moved to a four-bedroom house in Kent as they awaited the arrival of their baby boy. The obstacles they had encountered imparted valuable insights into the complexities of relationships, the importance of faith, and the power of determination. Now, they were ready to face the future as a united front, regardless of what it might bring uncertainties.

Afolabi's career continued to thrive, and his exceptional leadership at work garnered the respect and admiration of his colleagues. Yetunde, too, discovered a sense of fulfillment in her nursing career. She now guides and supports younger nurses while actively contributing to community health initiatives. Both individuals derived great satisfaction from their careers, recognizing that their dedication not only supported their loved ones but also had a positive impact on the lives of others.

As their daughters matured, Afolabi and Yetunde made it a point to pass on the principles that had shaped their own paths—strength, compassion, and the significance of kinship. Dara, Dami, and Damola were flourishing, their unique personalities blooming as they explored their passions and forged new connections. The family spent weekends immersing themselves in the beauty of the countryside, delving into the world of art at museums, and embracing the vibrant spirit of their community, creating unforgettable memories that would last a lifetime.

One day, while they were sitting in the living room, Dara, who had just turned ten, posed a question that surprised her parents. "Mum, Dad, could you share your experience of when you first arrived in the UK?" Was it challenging?"

Afolabi and Yetunde exchanged glances, their expressions softening. The parents recognised that their daughters had reached an age where they could understand certain difficulties they had faced. They aimed to be honest without overwhelming them with excessive information.

"It was certainly a test of my abilities," Afolabi began, carefully choosing his words. There are numerous challenges when adjusting to a foreign country, embracing unfamiliar customs, and forging a new life. However, our companionship was the key factor that distinguished us. We knew that regardless of the circumstances, we would face them united front."

Yetunde nodded, acknowledging the moments of fear and uncertainty about what lay ahead. "However, our firm faith in our love and the resilience of our family never wavered. And look at us now—we've created a beautiful life here, and we're incredibly proud of the three of you for being a part of that journey.

The children were captivated, their eyes filled with awe. The realisation dawned on them that their parents' love had endured countless trials, deepening their appreciation for their family.

As the evening came to an end, the family gathered around the dinner table, exchanging tales and enjoying each other's company. The room was filled with undeniable warmth and love, clearly reflecting their deep connection.

As time went on, Afolabi and Yetunde remained dedicated to their personal development and nurturing their bond. They opened a charitable organisation to support new couples and immigrants. They also became more engaged in their community, offering their time to local events and lending support to initiatives that helped other immigrant families adjust to life in a new country.

Once filled with obstacles and doubt, their love story transformed into a narrative of strength, dedication, and optimism. They understood that life would always have its highs and lows, but they had a firm belief in their capacity to confront any challenges that arose, united as a family one.

Legacy of Love

Over time, Afolabi and Yetunde witnessed their daughters' remarkable growth, filling them with pride. These young women exuded confidence and displayed genuine compassion for others. Dara thrived in her academic pursuits and cultivated a deep love for science. Meanwhile, Dami effortlessly showcased her artistic abilities, dedicating countless hours to creating beautiful drawings and paintings, while Damola took after his father to become an IT guru.

The family's home buzzed with joy, imagination, and the never-ending activity of daily existence. Afolabi and Yetunde continued to nurture their bond, never underestimating the affection that had carried them through numerous challenges. They had become a source of inspiration and support for each other and their children, who admired their steadfast strength and dedication.

On one warm summer evening, as they relaxed on the porch, Afolabi glanced at Yetunde with a pensive expression. "You know, Yetunde, I've been contemplating the future and the kind of impact we want to have on our children's lives."

Yetunde beamed, her heart filled with affection for the man who had been there for her through all the ups and downs. "I've been thinking about that too," she responded. "It's important for our children to understand that love encompasses more than just the happy moments. It's all about enduring the storms together, providing mutual support, and growing more resilient in the face of adversity." adversity.

Afolabi nodded, gently grasping her hand. "Exactly." He wanted their children to be reminded that, regardless of their challenges, they could conquer them through the strength of love, faith, and unwavering determination. He also wanted them to understand that they would always be there for them, just as they had supported one another.

They enjoyed a peaceful moment together, basking in the serene beauty of the sky as it transformed into a breathtaking display of colours. In that moment, a profound sense of tranquillity and satisfaction washed over them, realising they had crafted a life brimming with affection, strength, and optimism.

As they gazed at the horizon, Afolabi and Yetunde recognised that their adventure was still ongoing. There would be new obstacles to overcome, exciting journeys to undertake, and unforgettable moments to create. However, they were prepared to confront any challenges that crossed their path, confident in the strength of their love to withstand any obstacles.

As the sun dipped below the horizon, Afolabi and Yetunde found solace in one another's presence, appreciating the life they had built side by side. After facing numerous challenges, their love emerged even stronger, more enduring, and more beautiful than ever before. They were certain, without any doubt, that their enduring love would serve as a timeless source of inspiration and guidance for their family, spanning countless generations.

Afolabi turned around and found himself seated alone in the living room, still fully dressed on the same couch where he had been in the evening, except for the thick stockings on his legs instead of shoes, a sure handiwork by his wife; everything else was the same.

"What a wonderful dream! So vivid and so real. I must have dozed off after sharing the story with my daughters." He smiled to himself, fully aware that even in solitude, the vividness of the dream was a treasure he could hold onto forever.

He stretched with a yawn and got to his feet, a deep sense of contentment settling over him.

The end

www.ingramcontent.com/pod-product-compliance
Lightning Source LLC
LaVergne TN
LVHW050028080526
838202LV00070B/6964